THE PRIVATE EYE ANNUAL 1998

EDITED BY IAN HISLOP

"I'm sure it was the Viagra that killed him"

Published in Great Britain by
Private Eye Productions Ltd
6 Carlisle Street, London W1V 5RG

© 1998 Pressdram Ltd
ISBN 1 901784 12 6
Designed by Bridget Tisdall
Printed in England by
Ebenezer Baylis & Son Ltd, Worcester

2 4 6 8 10 9 7 5 3 1

THE PRIVATE EYE ANNUAL 1998

EDITED BY IAN HISLOP

The Daily Telegraffion

FINAL Britain's biggest-selling quality daily Friday, October 17, 1997 **45p**

Ffew! What A Tory!

by Our Political Staff Charles Phworr

TOP Conservative Ffion Jenkins today showed off her beautiful new fiancé Mr William Hhaaag to a rapturous Blackpool audience.

Miss Jenkins, who has united the party with her radical new dress, today outlined her vision of a new style of conservatism — young, modern and attractive. But this message, worthy as it is, has been overshadowed by her stunning new partner who has dazzled the Tory Die-Hards with his glamorous suits and upmarket sex appeal.

The Daily Telegraffion

Mr Hague's Good Start

MR WILLIAM Hague, in his first conference as Conservative leader, has firmly established himself as the guardian of genuine Conservatism. In his several speeches he repeatedly spelled out the same message, and it was one with which no traditional Tory could possibly disagree. The party, he said, must put the past behind it, and look to the future. Above all, he said, the Conservative Party must be popular. It must be modern-minded, attuned to the needs of today's world and also tomorrow's, rather than those of yesterday. Nothing was to be gained, he went on, by refighting the battles of the past. The party must above all be united.

The Conservative Party, Mr Hague emphasised, must appeal to all sections of the community — black people, young people, female people, disabled people, gay people, Village People, Pan's People, M. People, Sunday People, the People's People.

In a phrase which will often be quoted again, he told his followers: "People who need people are the luckiest people in the world, and that has to be our watchword if we are to be the popular, united, modern party that is going to lose the next election".

© Charles Moore, Age 97.

Hague wows Conference with See-Through Address

by Our Fashion Staff Alexandra Dulman

MR WILLIAM Hague delighted supporters when he turned up at Blackpool with a flimsy speech, which everyone could see through and which left nothing to the imagination.

Inside

How Should We Commemorate Diana, Princess of Wales?

We print a selection from the 58,000,000 letters sent in by our readers.

"It appears from our records that you haven't bought the Elton John single"

... may I suggest that the whole of the M1 should be turned into a permanent flower garden?

Mrs Enid Nutter, Brize Norton

... my idea is for Heathrow Airport to be renamed Her Royal Highness Diana, Princess of Wales Airport.

W. Hague, House of Commons

... what more fitting tribute could there be than to rename the Millennium Dome the Di-llennium Dome?

Mr Cyril Growbag, Burgess Hill

... may I suggest that the words of Elton John's wonderful song, Candle in the Wind, should be set in stained glass and placed in the East Window of Westminster Abbey?

Rev Nigel Gokart, Kidderminster

... surely there is only one fitting way to remember the Queen of All Our Hearts — to rename the days of the week in her memory, i.e. Sun-di, Mon-di, Tues-di etc.

Miss Teresa Clingfilm, Isle of Sheppey

... surely the most appropriate way to commemorate the People's Princess must be to replace the Queen's head with Diana's on all our coinage and banknotes? This way she will always be with us...

Lady Brenda Toast, Chipping Campden

... surely we as a nation should show our gratitude to Diana's brother for having the courage to speak out on behalf of the ordinary people of Britain. My suggestion is that he be made an Earl...

Mrs Boris Guppy, Eton

... how many of your readers recall that in ancient times Diana was the Goddess of the Moon? From now on, why don't we call the Moon 'the Diana'?

Sir David Frostrup, Weston-super-toseeyou

... why don't they coin a commemorative medal to be presented by the Queen to all those millions who queued (many for up to ten hours) to sign the books of condolence or to lay flowers in tribute to the most wonderful woman in history — its title, of course, the O.D.E. (the Order of Diana's Empire).

Mr E.R. Dafte, Chelmsford

... may I suggest that Remembrance Day should be rededicated to the memory of the Princess, rather than the dead of two world wars who are no longer relevant to modern Britain...

Prof. Stephen Ketchup, Manchester

And still the suggestions roll in. If you have any ideas to fill our pages, however ridiculous, please send them in, by letter, fax or email, because after two weeks we are desperate.

Every week **Dave Spart**, co-chair of the Crouch End Branch of the Republicans For Diana Movement, writes on the story behind the news.

THE Floral Revolution will totally go down in history as the most important display of the power of the British proletariat against the entrenched forces of the capitalist Establishment since the... er... Royal Wedding... and, er... there can only be one conclusion to the stunning victory of the masses over the reactionary monarcho-fascists of the Windsor family, ie that the sickening so-called Royal Family is totally and utterly finished and that a new political era has been born out of the ashes of the old coalition of aristocratic landed interest and, er... Earl Spencer spoke for the entire working class when he said that the Windsor dynasty was totally doomed and if proof were needed of that verdict the massed voices of the ordinary people sang "God Save The Queen" er... *(continued page 94)*

SPENCER vs WINDSOR

The young Princes should not be brought up by a man who was unfaithful to his wife while she was suffering from an eating disorder... Still, I'll have a go

6

DIANA'S FRIEND DIES

by Our Man in Calcutta
Lunchtime O'Vershadowed

AN ELDERLY nun who was once photographed shaking hands with the late Princess of Wales has died.

The nun first met Diana during the course of the Princess's work amongst the sick and dying and was apparently greatly inspired by her example.

Mother Teresa, as she was called, set up a mission to the poor of Calcutta which often ran into controversy, not least because of her lack of medical training and attempts to offer the downtrodden "love" rather than social justice.

However, despite these failings and a suspicion that the elderly nun enjoyed jetting around the world meeting famous people, she was judged to have been worthy of Princess Diana's friendship.

Her state funeral in Calcutta was a quiet event and was suitably low-key, so as to avoid any presumptuous similarities with that of Diana who is already being considered for canonisation by *(That's enough. Ed.)*

© The Times

LES BARTON

DID THE PRESS OVERKILL DIANA?

A special 94 page special by our Infill Team led by Phil Space

WERE newspapers guilty of hounding the Diana story to death in order to make money for themselves?

This is the question that must be urgently addressed by the press — particularly in the light of new evidence that has emerged in the last two weeks.

● **The papers were far too fast in bringing out memorial issues and were recklessly pursuing any angle in order to fill the pages.**

● **One reporter was going at 120 pieces a week. He was out of control and probably drunk. He should never have been in charge of a wordprocessor.**

● **Even when the story was clearly dying, journalists kept on taking pictures and writing features.**

● **The press deliberately impeded efforts to get over the tragedy by carrying on with their business.**

The case against the newspapers is overwhelming and newspaper editors have been told they must put their house in order.

"We have learned our lesson," said one chastened Fleet Street veteran. "We are all guilty of doing this story to death. We all have money on our hands."

And Still They Came

by Phillipa Column

It is now a week since the funeral and still they come. Tribute after tribute piles up in the newspapers as from all over the country thousands of columnists are moved to offer their views on the death of the Princess. Most of the pieces are short 1,000-word messages — and they are delivered by young and old alike. Many are badly written, hastily put together and childish in their sentiments. But they all asked the same unanswerable question, "Is this enough?".

And Still They Came

It is now a week and a day since the first few pieces began to appear at the front of the paper, but the tide of words shows no sign of abating. The air is heavy with the smell of humbug as the flowery prose mounts up at *(continued on all other pages for 94 days)*

St Cakes School

Diana Term begins today. As a mark of respect there are 149 boys in the school and 174 girls. As another mark of respect this announcement has been curtailed as any advertisement of the school's activities in the coming term has been deemed inappropriate by the Board of Governors (chairman Lord Crocodile O.C.). There will be a daily performance of "Candle in the Wind" (Words B. Taupin, Music E. John) in the chapel. It has also been agreed that the school should be re-dedicated as The Princess Diana Independent School for Boys and Girls (Formerly St Cakes). The following masters have been entered in the Paedophile Register: Mr R.C. Mackintosh, Rev P.J. Internet, and Major C.C.F. Gropelad.

'DIANA WROTE MY BOOK' MORTON TELLS ALL

by Andrew Morton (as told to himself)

WHY AM I revealing Diana's involvement with my book at this sad time? The answer is simple. Future historians and constitutional experts will need to gain a deeper insight into the troubled life of Princess Diana. These scholars will not be helped by the sudden flood of books purporting to tell the truth about the most important woman who had ever lived.

It is outrageous that these charlatans and ghouls should try and cash in on Diana's death. That is a task for myself.

Copies of my book, with the astonishing new section showing how Diana corrected my original text, are now available at all good bookshops or write to me personally (cash only). Andrew Mortonsofmoney, c/o Michael O'Moramoney, Moneysville, UK.

That Morton manuscript in full

> and that was it.
> It did not take Diana long to realise that Charles was a ~~problem~~. *bastard* Under the veneer of old world charm, the Prince of Wales was a wilful and selfish ~~man~~ who was neglecting his *bastard* new bride.
> As the months passed, the ~~Prince~~ *bastard* ~~of Wales~~ spent more and more time away from Highgrove with his ~~painting and his flowers.~~ *boot-faced old floozie.*
> The honeymoon was well and truly

> Meanwhile Diana was getting *more self-* ~~sadder~~ *stronger* and ~~lonelier~~. Unlike the *confident* Prince, she had ~~few~~ *many* intellectual interests to keep her occupied through her days. But her love of ~~clothes~~ *opera* and ~~shopping~~ *ballet* sustained her.

HAGUE: SCOTTISH REFERENDUM

> I'm a bit of a No-No

BSE INQUIRY TEAM

PERCIVAL

Notes & Queries

QUESTION. What is the correct pronunciation of "Althorp"? There seems to be some confusion about this. — *D. Dimbleby, White City*

☐ TREVOR McDonald is quite wrong in claiming that Althorp should rhyme with "Jeremy Thorpe". Althorp derives from the Anglo-Saxon words "All tripe", meaning a nobleman who gets above himself and talks a lot of pious and hypocritical cant about "family values" when his own record in this respect is less than edifying. The correct pronunciation is "humbug" — *Mrs Van der Kaffirbasher, Capetown.*

QUESTION. Who is Ben Pimlott? We seem to hear a lot about him these days, but I have yet to meet anyone who knows who he is. — *Mrs Cynthia Pimlott (no relation), Tufnell Park*

☐ ANTONIA Holden is quite wrong in suggesting that Ben Pimlott is the Queen's third-cousin, twice removed, by marriage to the fourth Duke of Fife. Ben Pimlott is in fact an anagrammatic pseudonym, concealing the identity of one of the leading writers and constitutional experts of our age, William Rees-Mogg. — *Will Hutton, Farringdon Road.*

QUESTION. We are told that there are now more than 23,000 Books of Condolence containing millions of signatures and tributes to the late Princess of Wales. Is it true that these are to be kept in the British Museum? — *Mrs Asda Safeway, Poundbury, Dorset*

☐ THE books are to be kept, but not in the British Museum. The latest plan is that they will all be put on display underneath the Millennium Dome. Here they will remain for at least a thousand years, under the constant supervision of teams of highly-trained archivists under the direction of Prof. Ben Pimlott. — *Chris Smith, Minister for Culture and the Media.*

QUESTION. What is the difference between Mr Sean Connolly and Mr Billy Connery? — *Mr Tam Dalyell, the Binn, West Lothian*

☐ THESE two leading experts on Scottish constitutional questions are often confused. One is a very boring rich actor who does not live in Scotland, and so is the other one. The way to tell them apart is that they both have beards, except for Brigitte Bardot. — *Prof. Norman Stone, Institute of Turkish Delight, Ankara's Aweigh.*

"Hello... yah, I'm on a train..."

Diana's Final Words

A statement by Michael Cole on behalf of the House of Fayed

I AM authorised by His Excellency King Mohamed Al Fayed to reveal exclusively to the world the final wishes of the late Princess of Wales.

Despite the denials of the hospital doctors, the French police, President Chirac, Diana's family and Her Majesty the Queen, I am pleased to inform you that the Princess *did* make a last statement whilst she was unconscious. These were her exact words:

"Tell the British Government to give Mohamed Al Fayed the fuggin' passport he so richly deserves."

M. COLE,
c/o Harrods House of Lies, Knightsbridge.

The Collected Letters and Speeches of Michael Cole are available in 3 volumes, in a special vellum-bound edition, from the Fayed Press, Alexandria. Only £2,500.

GLENDA SLAGG

The Columnist of Hearts

STEPHEN Fry — aren'tchasickof-him?! Some people may be Wilde about his Oscar (Geddit!?) but not me mister!?! How much more do we have to read about the celibate celeb, a-cruisin' and a-boozin', a-thievin' and a-grievin', a-whingein' and a-gringein' *(What that? Ed)*. Take a tip from Auntie Glenda, Stevie — put a cork in it! (I mean your mouth stoopid) and Zeebrugge off! (Geddit!?)

STEPHEN Fry — don'tchaluvhim? We're just Wilde about his Oscar!? (Geddit?!) And his new book had me leapin' and a-weepin' with laughter and tears!? Thank Gawd our Stephen has found happiness at last with his new live-in lover! Let's hope he keeps our Mr Brainbox on the straight and narrow — relatively speaking!? Geddit?? Carry on Jeeves!! Even if you are a Bertie Wooftah!?

STEPHEN Fry — don'tchafeel-ratherambivalentabouthim?! On the one hand he's very clever and funny, on the other hand haven't we read rather a lot about his private life recently? (You're fired. This is far too sensible. Ed)

HATS OFF to Mick Jagger!? OK, so he's old enough to be William Hagues's grandad!? Who isn't?! Whilst others are drawing their pension Mick is drawing huge crowds! Whilst they are getting on the Dial-a-ride, he's on the tour bus!? Thank Gawd Mick is still strummin' and a-hummin', a-bopping and a-hopping, a-jumpin' and a-humpin' *(This is terrible. You're hired again. Ed.)*

ROLLING Stone Mick Jagger?!! Looks more like a wrinkled old walnut to me!? For Gawd's sake Grandad, jumpin' jack it in and Jagger off (Geddit??) *(This is worse than McKay. Have a rise. Ed.)*

HERE they are: Glenda's Brighton Belles!
Severiano Ballesteros — give us a hole in one Señor Mister!! And I'll give you a Ryder any day!! (Geddit?!)

JONATHAN AITKEN — he's trying to stop the Arabs flogging some western girls!? That's *his* job!!? And he likes the flogging too!! (Geddit?!)

Simon Sebag Montefiore — crazy name, completely mad guy!

Byeeeeeee!!!

Alan Clark's History of the Conservative Party

Part 94: The Alan Clark Years

(Shot of man in agreeable suit standing on top of agreeable castle)

Clark *(for it is he)*: What could be more agreeable than this agreeable castle? Yet it was here that the seeds were sown of the destruction of the entire conservative party.

(Elgar-style music plays over black and white film of John Major being stumped during cricket match on village green in Brixton)

Clark: This hopeless little bank manager with his ghastly voice and ill-fitting underwear from Marks and Spencer was quite unfit to step into the shoes of Winston Thatcher. Surely the leader the party so desperately needed was this man? *(Hallelujah Chorus plays over black-and-white footage of Alan Clark chasing female BBC researcher in tight skirt round castle. Man in glasses appears with caption "Political Historian. Please don't switch off")*

Historian *(for it is he)*: Alan Clark had all the qualities to make him a first-class Prime Minister. He was charismatic, clever, wealthy and owned a large castle. Is that OK, Alan? Or shall I do it again?

(Cut back to Clark striding around countryside with rottweiler carrying BBC journalist's leg in its mouth)

Clark: Clark's finest hour came when he single-handedly defied his own government's guidelines by selling huge amounts of arms to Saddam Hussein. *(Holst-style music plays over film of Gulf War showing British soldiers under attack from British missiles. Cut back to Clark who goes off script and begins to foam at mouth)* And would you believe it, all the bloody pinkos and nig-nogs and chaps who didn't go to Eton made a bloody stink about it and brought down the whole government. *(Clark goes back to script after producer hits him over head with bottle of Mouton Rothschild 47)* This defeat allowed into power the greatest Conservative of them all — Tony Blair.

(Cut to Lord Deedes sitting in Canary Wharf playing Nintendo Golf Boy)

Deedes: I first met Disraeli in 1832. I had just become a cub reporter on *The Empire Clarion (continued for several weeks)*

"Shall we paint the town peach?"

Why Give These Exhibitionists The Publicity They Crave?

asks Brian R. Sewell

THERE IS only one reason why the Royal Academy is staging the most degraded, talentless, vulgar, voyeuristic exhibition of ghastliness in the history of the world — to drum up publicity.

The correct response from all sane, sensible, civilised commentators such as myself is to deny the exhibition organisers the one thing they crave — acres of attention from the press.

Clearly, what they want is for some unthinking, gullible art critic to devote the whole of his column to attacking the sheer horrible pointlessness of their tawdry and infantile efforts.

For example no one should waste any space at all writing about the particularly offensive exhibit in Room 45, Patric Mildew's Dead Chicken Foetus In A Condom With Crucifix (Bosnia '95).

Who in their right mind would even want to admit that they had paused for a moment in front of this naked example of onanistic self-promotion?

Surely we should all ignore the utterly repulsive video by Andrea Gromek showing a close-up sequence of herself urinating over a dead cat?

But perhaps the most offensive, degraded and narcissistic image in the entire exhibition is a picture of Mr Charles Saatchi entitled Our

Sponsor, which hangs in the foyer with the caption "Charles Saatchi Welcomes You To The Royal Academy".

I am glad to say that nothing on earth would persuade me to devote even a sentence to this pitiful vacuum of self-referential garbage.

On Other Pages

ART WORLD ROCKED BY EARTHQUAKE TRAGEDY

by Our News Staff **Tremor Macdonald**

ART lovers were in shock yesterday at the terrible news that an earthquake had not hit the Royal Academy, not causing the destruction of the entire Saatchi collection of modern art.

"It is a tragedy of inconceivable proportions," said one expert. "All the works are intact. There are no cracks anywhere in the paintings. None of the sculptures have been buried under rubble and the building is still safe enough for people to go and see the Exhibition."

There are fears of no more earthquakes in the coming days with the possibility of seismic activity measuring 0 on the Richter Scale.

Not Worth A Giotto

Tourists are warned that in this event they should avoid the Royal Academy at all costs and travel to Italy instead.

"Assisi may be a pile of rubble," said a critic, "but it's a lot better than this disaster zone."

Cimabue is 757.

Jeff Bernard
A nation mourns

by **David Dimbleby, Trevor Macdonald, Will Hutton, Richard Kay, Paul Dack, Andrew Marr, Ben Pimlott, Jeffrey Archer, Paul Johnson, Alan Rusbridger, John Simpson, Lord Archer, Lady Antonia Holden, Penny Junor, Hugo Vickers, Lord St John of Fawsley, Lord Blake, Stephen Glover, Ann Leslie, Anne McElvoy, Anne Appelbaum, Claire Rayner, Dr Thomas Stuttaford, Dr Raj Persaud, Lynda Lee-Potter, Charles Moore** and the **Staff of the Daily Hellograph** (That's enough names. Ed).

Jeff Bernard is dead.

The very words seem unreal.

As we write, it is impossible to take in the sheer enormity of what has happened.

In years to come everyone will remember exactly where they were when they heard the news that Jeff Bernard was no more.

There has never been a moment in history like it.

As the news sank in, millions of ordinary people flocked to his official residence in the heart of London, the Coach and Horses, Soho, to pay their last respects.

In the street outside, a mighty carpet of empty bottles stretched hundreds of yards in every direction, as a wordless tribute to the man they called simply "The People's Pisshead".

One man I spoke to was speechless, so overcome was he by the heady fumes of a thousand vodka bottles.

"I cannot speak," he said. "Jeff had the common touch. It was common for him to touch anyone in sight for the price of a gin and tonic..."

Meanwhile, the jukebox in the Coach and Horses was quietly playing the song by Elton John specially adapted in special tribute to the most loved and revered figure the pub has ever known.

Canned In The Pub
by Elton John Thribb

So. Goodbye Jeff Bernard
You were always in the pub.
But sometimes you were barred,
And couldn't get your grub.

And it seemed to me you lived your life
Like a candle on the bar
When there's been a power cut
And no one can see where they are.

Goodbye Jeff Bernard
You will be forever missed
In England's green and pleasant pubs
You were always pissed.

SACK ME OR I SQUIT

(surely 'Quit'? Ed.)

Hague's Shock Challenge

by Our Political Staff
Lobby Purves

VICKY WHEELER

MR William Hague, 17, who is believed to be the leader of the Tory Party, last night issued a challenge to his party over the issue of whether he should share a room at the Tory Conference with his fiancée Ffioncée Jenkins (formerly Lord Jenkins of Hillhead).

Mr Hague told Radio Five's popular early hours show "Is Anyone Awake?" that he proposed to make the sharing-the-room issue a test of his leadership at the Party Conference.

"I want a forward-looking, moderate Conservative Party that believes in pre-marital intercourse in hotel rooms," he said.

Mr Hague plans to put his radical new bedroom initiative to a referendum among the Tory Party's grass roots activists (Sid and Doris Parkinson).

But it is a high-risk strategy for Squitt.

Bring Back Major

If the Party decides not to back him, then he will have to stay on because there is no one else.

Last night, right-wing opposition to the "two in a bed" policy was hardening around the senior figure of former Tory leader Lady Thatcher.

"When I said that Hague was an ideal leader for the Party," she told close friends (Sid and Doris Powell), "what I meant was, he is a hopeless little squit, and the sooner he goes the better."

Lord Jenkins is 103.

"Stop thief! I want to apologise to you on behalf of the uncaring society that has made you what you are…"

A Taxi Driver writes

Every week a well-known cab driver is invited to comment on an issue of topical importance. This week: "The Saudi Nurses" by **Dave Mellor** (cab no. 47126).

Blimey, guv. You got to hand it to them Saudis. They got the right idea, haven't they? No messing about with trials and lawyers, eh? They clearly did it. So there's only one thing for it — string 'em up, or behead 'em. And 500 lashes into the bargain. Quite right too. None of our business to interfere. Their ways are not our ways. And who's to say that's wrong? Don't get much crime out in the desert, do you? Is it Riyadh or is it Dubai? Anyway, I 'ad one of their sheikhs in the back of my cab once. A very nice gentleman. Gave me a very generous tip — £500,000.

NEXT WEEK: Sir Paul Maccabbie (cab no. 4172) on Why Pop Music Is A Load Of Rubbish Nowadays.

"Gun control? Over my dead body…"

That Labour Conference Agenda in full

Day One
Unemployment — solved.

Day Two
Northern Ireland — peace achieved.

Day Three
Europe — sorted.

Day Four
Education — fixed.

Day Five
Health Service — reformed.

Day Six
Tony saw that it was good.

Day Seven
Tony rested.

OUTRAGE OVER FLOGGING

by Our Saudi Arabian Staff **Alan Koran and Lyn Barbarous**

WORLDWIDE opinion hardened last night at the decision by the British Government to carry on with its barbaric practice of flogging arms to Saudi Arabia.

Appeals to Britain fell on deaf ears as a resolute British government spokesman told reporters. "You don't understand our country. This is our way. We have been flogging for centuries. It is a fundamental part of our culture and we are not going to stop just because everyone thinks it's uncivilised."

A fanatical member of the business community said: "It is written in the books. Arms must be flogged or else we won't make any money. It could not be clearer."

Al-anclark

There were, however, a few international defenders of Britain's ancient customs. A Mr Saddam Hussein from Iraq went on the record saying: "I was flogged arms by Britain on a number of occasions and it didn't do me any harm. In fact, I learned my lesson, ie I could do whatever I liked."

A Mr Suharto from Indonesia agreed: "I was publicly given 500 of the best; the best anti-personnel aircraft on the market. And I respect Britain for that."

Meanwhile, Robin Cook *(continued p. 94)*

WHO SHOULD PLAY PRINCESS DI IN THAT NEW FILM?

'PASSIVE SMIRKING'

New danger says report

by Our Health Staff
Dr Thomas Utterfrau

IN AN astonishing new survey released last night, doctors claim that even people who do not smirk themselves could be seriously harmed by "passive smirking".

"Even being in the same room as Richard Branson is dangerous," says the report.

"Branson may be opening a bank posing in bed with Chris Evans or turning a Spice Girl upside down. But whatever he is doing his smirking habit can cause you immediate irritation and in the end it will get right up your nose.

The report concludes: "This may lead to nausea and even death." *(Cont. p.94)*.

WE AT the Daily Moron say that you, the people, should choose who you want to play your People's Princess in the Hollywood blockbuster that is coming to your local cinema soon — *One Wedding And A Funeral*.

It is only right and proper that the British people should have the final say when it comes to casting the most important movie role ever.

Should it be?

1. Liz Hurley
2. Melinda Messenger
3. Ulrika Jonsson
4. Carol Vordemann
5. The Spice Girls
6. Jodi Foster
7. Sharon Stone
8. Madonna
9. Eddie Izzard
10. Peregrine Worsthorne

Phone now on the Moron Royal Hotline 0800 62461. All calls free (38p a second).

BLAIR MEETS YELTSIN

You're not much of a socialist

ARRIVALS

N.T.C. T.V. — JC CHEMICAL — DrUGS PICKUP

GLENDA SLAGG
Fleet Street's Waste of Spice!!!

SHED A TEAR for poor Jane Asher who's lost her job selling biscuits and cakes on the telly!?!! Jus' cos she ain't a teenager no more!?!! Well, Mister, that really takes the biscuit (geddit?!) Everyone knows she's still a cracker (geddit??!!) and you can't just fire someone for being too old can you!?!!! *(Yes. You're fired. Ed.)*

GOOD riddance to Jane Asher!? About time, too, ginger nut (Geddit??!) Two chocolate fingers to you!!?? Now you can spend more time hob-knobbing with cuddly hubby cartoon king Gerry!?!!! Crumbs!?! *(This is terrible. You're hired again. Ed.)*

THREE cheers for the gorgeous Gallagher Brothers who woke up boring old Radio One with their stream of drug-filled obscenities!?!!

But what's all the fuss about, Auntie?!

Surely what we all need is more of the Oasis boys a-fuggin' and a-druggin' on our trannies?!!! Not less!!

These two swearing swingers have really put Britain back on top of the obscenity charts!?!!!

Let's have your next single lads — All You Need Is Fuggin' Heroin!?!!

MICHAEL SCHUMACHER!?!! Aren'tchasickofhim??!! Typical German!?! As soon as he thinks he's lost the race he tries to murder his opponent?!!! But he got his come-uppance just like they did in 1914-1918, in 1939-45 and in 1966!? The World Cup, Mister, in case you forgot!!! Clear off to your bunker,

Fritz, take your crashed Kraut car with you *(It was a Ferrari, Ed.)* and don't forget the cyanide pills!??

That's my Formula One for getting rid of you!? (Geddit?!?)

HATS OFF to Mad Mike Schumacher!? OK, so he tried to kill his opponent? So what?! I like a man who puts his foot on the throttle and doesn't care who he hits!! What a Villeneuve of the whingeing Frenchman *(He was a Canadian, Ed.)* to complain??! Jacques it in!!?! (Geddit?!)

HERE they are – Glenda's November Bangers!

PIERS MERCHANT. You can come round and research the excesses of the British tabloids at my place any time!!??! And don't forget to bring your wife!?!

CLIFFORD WILLIAMS — The Randy Reverend to you, Mister!!??! It's his hornier-than-thou attitude that I like!! Geddit?!?!

EMEKA ANYAOKU, Commonwealth General Secretary. Crazy name, crazy guy!!?!

Byeeeeee!

12

"Stop complaining, Johnson, and just be thankful this class is below average size"

Autumn Books

Had Enough Yet?
by Nicola Borlick

THE incredible true-life story of a woman who works in a bank, has some children and still finds time to write a book about how marvellous she is. Macmillions, 999 pages, £25.99 *(Serialised in the Daily Telegraph and all other papers.)*

I Was Better Than Spiggy
by Sir Paul Macitallupney

THE former Turd tells in his own words how brilliant he was and how everyone else in the group was useless, especially Spiggy Topes, even though he wrote all the hits including "I'm a

Red Hot Swinging Perve". Sackem and Gasbag, 999 pages, £37.99

Harry Thompson
by the late Peter Cook

AUTHOR Cook charts in remorseless detail the sad story of the brilliant comedy producer Harry "Toppo" Thompson who takes London by storm and then leaves his wife and children to live with Victoria Coren. From the heady days of "Have I Got Bad News For You, Darling," the book charts Thompson's relentless decline, due to his addiction to women, until he is reduced to the final indignity of producing the down-market indoor sports quiz *They Think It's All Legover.* Allcock and Tweed, £49.99

APOLOGY
From The Conservative Party

IN the last 18 years, not to mention the last 800, we in the Conservative Party may have inadvertently given the impression that we were in some way in favour of stringing up the following:

● **Blacks**
● **Gays**
● **Foreigners**
● **Single Mothers**
● **The Unemployed**
● **Members of the Labour Party**
● **Blacks**
● **Anyone else who was not one of us.**

This unfortunate public perception of the Conservative Party in no way accorded with the facts but may have been assisted by the misinterpretation of conference speeches by leading figures urging Conservatives to string up the following:

● **Gay Foreigners**
● **Unemployed Blacks**
● **Guardian Readers**
● **Pinko Single Mothers**
● **Etc**

We would now like to make it clear that the Conservative Party has always been the party of tolerance, compassion and caring towards those not privileged enough to be white, heterosexual members of the Conservative Party who read the Telegraph.

We would also like to stress that any member of the party that does not share these beliefs is an unreconstructed dinosaur who should be strung up as soon as we can get capital punishment reintroduced.

> Lord Gnome
> New Conservative Central Office
> Tolerance House
> John Smith Square
> London

"I don't think he's quite got the hang of our new image"

Three Taxi Drivers write

For the first time ever we invite no fewer than three prominent cab drivers to comment on all the important issues of the day.

'Normo' Tebbs (Cab No. 876) on the multi-cultural society

I've got nothing against them personally. Don't get me wrong. But if they come over here, they've got to learn our ways. They've got to assumulate… astimulate… assomol… you know, fit in. We've got our British culture which goes back thousands of years, football, EastEnders, Chris Evans, curry houses, Frank Bruno. And they've got to accept it, like everyone else. I mean, it's just like the poofs, isn't it? They're not the same as us, guv, are they? You know what I'd do with them? The blacks, the gays, the Asians, the Urdus. I'd send them back where they come from. It's the only language they understand, 'cos they certainly don't speak English, do they? Not like wot you and I can. I 'ad that Justin Fashanu in the back of the cab once. Very nicely spoken, 'e was. A proper gentleman.

'Al' Clark, (Saltwood Car Hire) on the Ulster Peace Process

Blimey, guv. You seen those talks they're still having in Northern Ireland? Waste of time, to my mind. Know what I'd do? Shoot the lot of them.

Everyone knows who they are. They know where they live. They should go round in the middle of the night and string 'em up. That would be the end of it. I 'ad this Brigadier from the SAS in the back of the cab once. He showed me all their addresses. Very nice gentleman he was too. I gave him a whole book of receipts.

Tony 'Banksie' Banks (Cab No.472) on the Conservative Leadership

Seen that new bloke the Tories have got? I'll tell you what he looks like. One of them foetuses that haven't been born. I'll tell you another thing, guv. I bet some of them Tory MPs wish they'd voted in favour of abortion. See what I mean? Do you mind not smoking, guv? I've got a non-smoking policy in this cab. See the match? I missed it, I was too pissed. I 'ad that David Mellor in the back of the cab once. A real gentleman. A pleasure to drive around.

(That's enough cabbies. Ed.)

"Oh dear… looks like the Kebab Wars have started again"

"We believe this one was around during the Ice Age"

The Conversion of St Paultillo

THERE WAS a young man in those days called Saultillo who persecuted those who were not like himself and failed to believe the orthodox religion of the time. No one was more dutiful than Saultillo in worshipping the Goddess (Thatchahweh) and smiting her enemies.

Then one day Saultillo was travelling to Blackpool on an Virgin Train which had stopped for several hours due to a shortage of drivers, carriages, trains, etc, after the recent privatisation.

And suddenly lo! there was a blinding flash and a voice said over the tannoy: "Saultillo! Saultillo! If you want to be the next Tory leader you'll have to stop persecuting people and change your tune, matey!"

Saultillo then opened his eyes with a jerk (William Hague) and found that he was still in Crewe.

And from that day forward Paultillo, as he became known, worked tirelessly on behalf of himself spreading the new message — "Vote For Paultillo".

NEXT WEEK: St Glenn of Hoddle (The Conversion of the Eleven Useless Men)

GLENDA SLAGG

On tour with Her Majesty The Queen

FOR cryin' out loud Ma'am — put a sock in it!?! Geddit!! Gawd help us?! What is the world coming to when the British Queen cannot afford a pair of shoes?! OK, the Monarchy needs to cut down on its expenses but you would have thought they could have run to a pair of shoes?!! Even a pair of trainers from Woolies would do!? Come on Phil! Put your hand in your pocket and fork out for the Missis!? We can't have all those Indians and Pakistanis a-sniggering up their saris whilst the Queen goes walkabout looking like a bag lady!?! Blimey!! Bring back Diana!?! *(You're fired. Ed.)*

"Are we there yet?"

BRITISH FASHION WEEK TAKES EASTBOURNE BY STORM

by Our Political Staff **Philuppa Page**

THE SLEEPY seaside town of Eastbourne was yesterday transformed into the world's fashion capital, as super-models flew in from all over Britain to launch designer Willy Hague's new "Britsquit"

Menswear Collection.

Said Hague: "I've gone for a sort of very 90s casual-but-compassionate feel. I'm calling it the 'washed-up' look".

Notably absent from the Eastbourne catwalk was outsize-

model 34-stone "Nikki" Soames, who last night told fashion editors: "I haven't got time to ponce about by the seaside with this ghastly little man. I'm too busy having lunch in my club." William Hague is 11.

Stevie Dorrell goes "Woolly"

Al Clark in "Stupid Country"

Johnnie Deadwood in "Drip-Dry Vulcan"

Hague modelling own designer "Jacket-In"

PRODUCT RECALL EXECUTIVE

MAZUKKE

15

CHARLES PRAISES 'ALTERNATIVE MONARCHY'

by Our Medical Staff **Lunchtime O'Listic**

PRINCE Charles yesterday called for the acceptance of an "alternative monarchy", which he hoped would finally replace the more conventional form.

Speaking from his organic trousers at Highgrove, Gloucs, the Prince explained "I'm not knocking traditional monarchy. For a lot of people, the orthodox approach of a woman in a twin-set and crown looking miserable and going on television once a year does the trick".

"It makes them feel better and there's nothing wrong with that."

"But nowadays more and more people are seeking an alternative form of monarchy."

"They want an organic, holistic, you know, homeopathic, aromatherapeutic, those needle thingies... wisdom of the east... wisdom of the yeast... a spoonful of sugar makes the live yoghurt go down... sort of monarchy, and I feel I can offer that."

When You Are Feeling Poorly, Which Approach Do You Favour?

Old-style Queen, or new-style Prince Charles? Call now on 01800-462462 or send messages telepathically *(entirely free).*

"What's Walter brought back with him this time?"

HISTORIC MEETING

Perhaps your wife could defend my wife?

You couldn't afford her fees old boy

Daily ⚜ Mail

The Paper You Can Trust

BLAIR LYNCHED BY CITY MEN

By Our Man In The City **Fred Needle**

THE PRIME Minister was lucky to escape with his life when he appeared on the floor of the Stock Exchange yesterday, according to an exclusive report by Daily Mail staff.

Angry dealers surrounded Tony Blair smiling with fury and began shouting: "Good old Tony, what are you doing for lunch?"

No wonder the Prime Minister apparently looked white as a sheet as he beat a hasty retreat after spending only two hours signing autographs.

Security men had their jobs cut out keeping murderous brokers from shaking Blair's hand and telling him they hoped he would be Prime Minister for many years to come.

Totally Untrue

It was one of the worst public relations disasters that the Daily Mail has ever made up *(shurely 'witnessed'? Ed).* No wonder the honeymoon is over and Labour are totally finished.

THE INDEscribablyworsethanever

Price: Given away on trains   Friday 31 October 1997

'The last leaf of autumn falls painfully to earth'

It is 6.32pm in an ordinary suburban street. A dog barks. An old woman is shuffling along the pavement, bent under the weight of her shopping.

Overhead there is the rumble of

BY WILL THISDO

a distant jet flying in from faraway Frankfurt or possibly Kuala Lumpur.

Oblivious of the scene below, Captain Collimore is informing passengers that ground temperature at Gatwick is "a pleasant 21 degrees Celsius" and that "local time is now 6.33pm".

A whole minute has passed. And it has taken all that time for a single leaf to fall from the branch of a London plane tree outside my offices.

It is a time of year for things to fall.

Leaves. Rain. The circulation of the Independent.

Has it got anything to do with the new-style front page? We shall never know.

Those 100 words that conjure up our century

From the Collins Dictionary (proprietor Rupert Murdoch)

Tit	**Panties**
Bum	**Vote Conservative**
Page Three	**Sky TV**
Corr	**Sizzling**
Gotcha	**Soaraway**
Bonk	**Kinky**
Spice Girls	**Boobs**
Melinda Messenger	**Times only 10p**
36-24-36	**Vote Labour**
Love Romp	*(continued for ever)*

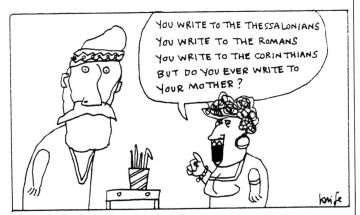

Saint Paul gets a visit

The Alternative Rocky Horror Service Book

No 94. Service For The Bedding Of Women

The Vicar (*for it is he*): Dearly beloved (especially you in the second row with the hat), as the scripture saith, when two or three are gathered together in bed, there am I in the midst of you, having a good time.

All: Ooh, you are a one! (or it may be "cheeky!", or some such appropriate response).

Vicar: I fancy something on the organ.

Organist: I will pull out all the stops.

All: Hark at her!

(The organist will then play a quick fugue in three parts)

Vicar: Just a few notices. There will be a ladies' house group tomorrow night at Mrs Naughtie's, because her husband is away on business. I shall be leading the discussion on the Church's role in Uganda.

(Hymn: No. 94 from the S and M Hymn Book, "Abed With Me". *Followed by* Reading: The Women Taken In Adultery. *There will then be a laying on of hands by the Vicar, when he will lay his hands on any female member of the congregation under the age of 80*)

The Obscene Creed

Vicar: I believe in One Bed, and the Three Persons in It. Amen.

Dismissal

The Bishop: You're fired.

THE PEOPLE'S THEATRE

(formerly the Royal Opera House and English National Opera)

P R E S E N T S

THE SPICE GIRLS

— I N —

THE TWILIGHT OF THE NOBS

— O R —

GUMMERDAMMERUNG

BESTIE

YOU'RE NO SON OF MINE GO TO HOLLYWOOD WHERE YOU BELONG.

UNFORTUNATELY PINK PANTHER'S FATHER WAS HOMOPHOBIC

— ACT ONE —

As the curtain rises, it is taken away by the bailiffs.

The stage is filled with squabbling aristocrats who are trying to decide who can waste the most money on the worst productions.

The Lords Chadlington and Gowrie sing the celebrated duet *Siamo due gitti inutile* ("We are a couple of useless gits").

They are joined by the Baroness Blackstone, Queen of the Nightmare, accompanied by the Three Harpies, Vivien Duffield, Genista Macintosh and Mary Allen.

They sing the celebrated *Catalogue Aria* from Don Jeremyisaacs, boasting about the amount of public money they have wasted over the years (*100 millione e tre*).

— ACT TWO —

Lord Chadlington comes on to explain his plan to build the largest opera house in the world covering the whole of Covent Garden.

A huge army of workmen enter and sing the *Overtime Chorus* before falling asleep.

Dancers and singers arrive at the Odeon bingo hall, Neasden, to perform

The Merry Widow and are surprised to find that nobody turns up, except Sid and Doris Bonkers who complain loudly that there is no bingo, in the duet *Sex und sechsig, clicketty-von-click* (On its own, number one).

— ACT THREE —

There is a trumpet call. Enter The Minister (Chris Smith) with his faithful Partner.

He is furious with Chadlington and Gowrie and sings the aria *Your tiny bank account is frozen.*

He then unveils his own plan to force both the opera companies into the People's Millennium Dome, where they will put on joint productions of such popular operas as *Cats, Starlight Express* and Walt Disney's *Beauty and the Beast.*

All ends happily when a large fluffy cloud appears, on which stands a group of anonymous, god-like donors, showering millions of pounds over everyone in sight. Lord Chadlington and Mary Allen lock in fond embrace and reprise the aria *Your Tiny Bank Account Is Now A Very Large One.* The Spice Girls then enter with Dame Kiri Te Kanawa and sing their latest best-selling aria *Madonna Is On Her Mobile.*

CHARITY SHOP   Refugee Relief   NEARLY NEW CLOTHES   J. JONES   HELP the HELPLESS   OX[

Stowell

"Oddly enough, I'm here to make a living for myself"

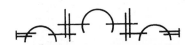

A Poirot Mystery

THE CASE OF THE FUGGIN' EMERALDS

by Agatha Christie

"FIRST Floor — Magazines, Magazine Subscriptions and Bargain Magazines." The uniformed attendant in the Harrods lift pronounced his litany with obvious boredom as Hercule Poirot, the famous Belgian detective, was conveyed to the penthouse suite of the world-renowned department store.

"So, 'Astings," Poirot observed to his companion, "zis is ze famous 'Arrods where you can buy anyzing from an elephant to a…"

"…a conservative MP?" ventured his faithful assistant, Colonel Hastings, with a smile.

"Quite so, 'Astings," replied the legendary sleuth, contemplating his latest case with pleasurable anticipation.

As the lift doors closed behind them, the two men were greeted by a strangely bouffant-haired figure, dressed in an electric-pink shirt.

"Good afternoon, gentlemen," he purred. "How very kind of you to come. My name is Michael Cole — you may have read some of my letters to the newspapers."

"Indeed, I 'ave, Monsieur. And most interesting zey were, too. I so much admire your… 'ow you say…"

"Honesty?" suggested the helpful factotum.

"…Non, monsieur, ze word I 'ad in mind was 'mendacité'."

Cole beamed. "You are too kind. But now I am instructed to take you into the presence of Mr Al-Fayed himself…"

"YOU CALLIN' me a fuggin' thief? You Belgian fuggin' poof!" The swarthy Egyptian entrepreneur thumped his fist on the imitation Louis XIX Chippendale mahogany escritoire.

Poirot's eyes narrowed with disdain, as Mr Cole hastened to clarify his employer's position.

"I think that what Lord Fayed wishes to say is that he had no knowledge of the so-called 'Lonrho emeralds' which Mr Rowland alleges he placed in a Harrods deposit box."

"And yet," the great detective intervened, twirling his waxed moustaches, "I 'ave here a signed statement from one of your own security staff zat Mr Fayed 'imself broke into ze box with ze 'ammeur, wearing special white gloves, and removed ze priceless gemstones 'imself. Is zat not so, 'Astings?"

"Fuggin' liar!" screamed the portly billionaire, resorting under stress to the argot of his native Port Said.

"'Astings, ze affidavit, if you would be so good?" said Poirot, turning to his right-hand man.

Hastings reached into an inside pocket and produced an imposing legal document.

"Do I have to read it?" he asked menacingly, looking across the desk at the now visibly flustered store-owner.

Mr Al-Fayed flapped irritably at his Head of Public and Corporate Relations, gesturing towards an oil painting of the Mona Lisa on the wall behind him.

Poirot watched fascinated as the dapper functionary operated a hidden spring-mechanism, and the painting swung aside to reveal a metal safe.

"Look," said Cole, "Earl Fayed wants you to know that there must have been some sort of a misunderstanding. He would like you to accept this small token of his esteem, to show that there are no hard feelings."

As he spoke he was turning the dial of the safe, first one way, then the other, with practised dexterity.

"Fuggin' 'urry up," snapped the impatient entrepreneur.

At last the door swung open to reveal large piles of neatly stacked brown envelopes.

As Cole pulled out a handful of them, he added in obsequious tones, "My employer is of course entirely innocent of any charges, and he is delighted you have agreed that this is an end to the whole unfortunate affair".

"Just give them the fuggin' money," snarled the world's most famous shopkeeper.

But Poirot's observant eyes were no longer on the brown envelopes being proffered to him by the egregious lackey.

"Regard, mon ami!" he exclaimed to Hastings, pointing with his cane to the back of the safe.

There, twinkling in the darkness, like little green stars, were what looked remarkably like a set of enormous emeralds.

"You fuggin' idiot, Cole," barked Fayed. "You're fired."

"I zink our little case is solved," concluded Poirot with a smile. "I shall be in contact wiz my friends at Scotland Yard in ze morning."

NEXT WEEK: Poirot investigates the mystery of The Missing Last Words of Princess Diana.

LET'S PARLER FRANGLAIS

avec Tony et Jacques!!

Numéro 94: Tony et Jacques go to le Canary Wharf.

Jacques Chirac *(pour c'est lui)*: Ah, Tony! C'est très moderne, la nouvelle Bretagne, n'est-ce pas!

Tony: Oui! C'est cool! C'est pivotal, c'est le nouveau brand de Royaume Uni!

Qu'est-ce vous reckon then?

Jacques Chirac: Nul points!! Ha ha ha! Et maintenant les marks pour le chanson Norwegien!

(Chirac sits on le sofa d'Habitat qui collapses immédiatement)

Tony: C'est just like votre government, n'est-ce pas? Ha ha ha!

Chirac: Le next time, je preferais Chequers, s'il vous plait. Les sofas sont beaucoup plus comfortables.

Tony: Ha! Vous n'êtes pas half as cool as nous Anglais. Nous sommes almost froid.
(Ça suffit, Reditor)

That Anglo-French Canary Wharf Summit Menu In Full

prepared by England's top chef **Tony Bulldog** (formerly Jean-Claude Botticelli von Heydseck)

Cream of Alastair Campbell's Soup

— ✳ —

Fillet of Emu (underdone) on a Sofa of Lettuce-In

— ✳ —

U Turnedos Steaks with New Labour Potatoes and a Jospin of French Has-Beans

— ✳ —

Blockade of Lamb with a Chirac of Jam Français

— ✳ —

Canary Wharffle with Fudge Sauce

— ✳ —

Conrad Black Coffee with Cherie Brandy

— ✳ —

Diners are reminded by the management that this is a first sitting and ministers are asked to vacate their tables within one hour to allow suitable profit to be made for Sir Terence Conman.

Smoking is compulsory in all areas.

The Alternative Rocky Horror Service Book

No. 94: A Service of Remembrance For All The Gay Servicemen and Women Who Are Already Remembered In The Original Service

President
(Peter Tatchell, for it is she): We shall start with a two-minute silence to remember the appalling way in which large numbers of servicemen and women were remembered purely for the fact that they gave their lives for their country and not for the fact that they were gay.

(Young men in leather jackets shall then respond with the following response)

All: Hullo sailor *(or it may be "Hullo soldier" or "Hullo airman")*.

(There will then be two minutes silence while the photographers take pictures of Peter Tatchell)

President *(reads)*: At the going down of the trousers, we shall remember them.

(Hymn: "The Gay Thou Gavest Lord Is Ended")

President: Remember, we wear our poppies with gay pride.

(The congregation shall then process to the Cenotaph in Whitehall to protest noisily during the official two minutes silence that neither Vera Lynn nor the Spice Girls are gay)

© St Peter of Tatchell 1997

"OK, so every month we choose a book, read it, then we meet up to discuss whether it should be burned"

Ten Tell-Tale Signs That Britain Is Cool

1. Tony Blair is cool.

2. Terence Conran's food is cool.

3. Body Shop is cool.

4. The Spice Girls are really cool.

5. England 0 Italy 0. Cool!

6. John Galliano sounds a cool guy, whoever he is.

7. Modern sofas are cool.

8. Cappuccino is cool, even though it's meant to be hot.

9. It's very cool for the time of year.

10. Don't cool us, we'll cool you.

Statistics compiled by The Central Office of Official Labour (COOL), P. Mandelson prop.

THE SUN SAYS

Is Louise Innocent?

You decide

Yes, she is — ring 0809 45267

Yes, she is — ring 0801 45268

Calls charged at 38p a second. All proceeds go to the Sun "Louise Is Innocent" fighting fund.

THE SUN ALSO SAYS

Sing A Song For Louise on Remembrance Day

Chuck your poppy in the bin, and put on a yellow ribbon instead. That'll show those bloodthirsty Yanks we've not forgotten our Queen of Nannies. The whole country is united, to sing with one voice the new national anthem:

Nanny In The Wind

Goodbye, English au pair.
Though I never knew you at all.
But I've seen you on the telly
And it made me want to bawl.
And it seems to me you lived your life
Like a nanny in the wind.
Etc. Etc.

© Elton Village

And The Sun Has Thought Of Something Else To Say

We say the Americans' treatment of Louise is so disgusting that prime minister Blair should send in the SAS to rescue Louise, whatever the loss of life that this would involve.

We must bring baby Louise home for Christmas with her loved ones.

● **American-owned products that you must boycott to show how much you care:**

1. **McDonald's Hamburgers**
2. **Coca Cola**
3. **Levi Jeans**
4. **The Sun newspaper**

Fox Fishing for Beginners

with Michael Foster MP, angler and anti-hunting protester

brian bagnall

1. Impale rabbit/chicken/pheasant on a large treble hook and place outside earth.

2. When fox takes the bait, play it for extended period by pulling it across country ("drag fishing").

Important Note

This sport is in no way cruel as proved by the millions of people in Britain who regularly fish and come from traditional Labour-voting backgrounds.

'I AM INNOCENT'
Briton's Desperate Plea

by Our Legal Staff **Joshua Rozenbeard**

THE WHOLE world was moved to tears of laughter yesterday by the continued campaign of the tragic British MP, Neil Hamilton, to clear his name.

Thousands of supporters did not attend a night-time vigil and no one wore yellow ribbons in an emotional display of solidarity with the 49-year-old British parliamentarian.

"I have done nothing wrong," sobbed Neil as the pressure mounted to lock him up for the rest of his life.

"Neil has not had a fair trial," claimed his close relative, Mrs Hamilton, "because he knew he would lose to the Guardian."

There have been no calls for a review of the British judicial system and legal experts are agreed that nothing must be done to overturn the guilty verdict.

Neil Hamilton is appealing to no one.

Join the Eye campaign to "Jail Our Neil"

Just send a cash donation at once in a brown envelope to Neil Hamilton, c/o Harrods.

PRE-RAPHAELITE BROTHERHOOD

PRE-RAPHAELITE SISTERHOOD

BBC 24 HOUR NEWS
What you missed

(Man in shirtsleeves with overworked staff in background trying to think of some news)

Gavin Essler: And the main news is that the BBC's 24 Hour News Service is up and running. Later in the programme we'll be looking at the early part of this programme and then we'll be giving you full details of the BBC's 24 Hour News Service. But first News Update with someone else.

Blonde Woman *(for it is she)*: The BBC has launched its first ever 24 Hour News Service. Speaking earlier on this channel, a BBC spokesman, Mr Gavin Essler, said that he could confirm that the BBC had indeed launched a 24 Hour News Service. We'll be talking to Mr Essler later in the programme. Gavin?

Essler: Thank you, blonde woman. The latest on the BBC 24 Hour News Service story… *(caption "LIVE")* …is that the service is on the BBC and it lasts for 24 hours. That's a whole day in any language.

Blonde Woman: Can you expand on that, Gavin, er… for maybe 24 hours?

(Viewer wakes up and turns off television)

©*24 Hour Birtnews* *("No News Is Our News")* If you have a news story that you would like Gavin Essler to read, e-mail us now at zzz.Birttosh.uk.co.zzz

---

"You don't think we're dumbing it down, do you Sooty?"

Issued by HM Government

NO MORE TESSAS – NOW IT'S THE GEOFFREY!

SAVERS

Announcing a new scheme to provide tax-free benefits for you and your family (but particularly you).

 THE GEOFFREY

HOW IT WORKS

■ Simply invest a minimum sum of 12 million pounds in an offshore trust in Guernsey or Bermuda.

■ Watch while tax-free money piles up for you and your loved ones!

It's so easy — and you don't even have to resign.

You can put your trust in a Geoffrey — and we'll be blind to it!

COURT CIRCULAR

SYDNEY, AUSTRALIA

The State Funeral took place today in St Edna's Cathedral, Sydney, of the late Sir Michael Hutchence INXS, who had lain in state for 24 hours pending an autopsy by Inspector Knackeroo of the New South Wales Illegal Substances and Auto-Erotic Activities Unit. The cortege was attended by Her Royal Highness the Kylie of Minogue, Dame Helena of Christensen and the Dowager Paula of Yates who read A Communication on the Blessed Bob Geldof, whom she described as being personally responsible for the demise of the deceased. She was accompanied by the Royal Infanta, the Heavenly Tiger Lily of Hiraani. The Archdeacon of Sydney, the Very Rev J.C. Flannelwanger, paid tribute to "this extraordinary talent, perhaps the greatest genius of his generation, whom I hadn't heard of until this morning" *(cont'd p 94)*.

Who Do You Blame For Pop Star's Tragic End?

You decide who was responsible for Michael Hutchence's death in the Sun's People's Jury (shortly to replace the official coroner in all civilised countries).

Was it:

a) **Bob Geldof?**

b) **Kylie Minogue?**

c) **Jonah Lomu?**

d) **The Teletubbies?**

e) **Rolf Harris?**

f) **The Spice Girls?**

g) **Michael Fish?**

h) **Himself** *(surely some mistake?)*

Phone NOW and waste someone's time! 0898752 347

As Seen On TV

Call My Duff

TWO teams of panellists try to guess the name of the famous TV producer whose wife Fiona Duff has rubbished him in the Daily Mail for running off with the daughter of a *Call My Bluff* star.

Chairman: And the first word is "Thompson".

Coren: Well, a "Thompson" is the sort of bloke who comes along looking perfectly innocent, and then, blimey, what do you know, he walks off with your daughter. I say, string him up. What a bastard. That's a "Harry".

(Other team all hold up cards saying "True")

"James has given up smoking recently!"

BACKBONE TO BE BANNED

Says Government

by Our Agriculture Staff **CJD Booker**

AGRICULTURE Minister Dr Jack Cunningham last night announced a total ban on "spines" in British Government.

"It is better to be safe than sorry," he explained, "and we are confronting a situation where some Labour MPs are showing distressing signs of having a backbone and not following the herd. They are clearly mad and should be taken out and culled.

"Safe MPs are easily distinguished by a yellow streak going through them. These pose no threat to anyone and can be eaten for breakfast by Tony Blair."

Moo Mowlam is 47.

Those Paxman Questions The Girls Couldn't Answer

by Our Universally Challenged Staff **Bambi Gasgoigne**

A RECORD poor performance was achieved last week by the girls of New Labour College, Westminster in an embarrassing fiasco presided over by TV's quizmaster Jeremy Paxman. The girls failed to give the correct answer to any questions at all. Here are some of those questions and the answers they gave:

Paxman: Why are you cutting single parent benefit?

Harman: Er... Posh Spice... er...

Paxman: Why did you change your policy on tobacco sponsorship of Formula One?

Jowell: Er... Beethoven's Fifth? Winston Churchill?

Paxman: Would you legalise cannabis?

Short: Yes... I mean no... er...

Paxman: Why is Gerry Adams coming over for Christmas?

Mowlam: Er... alpha rays... parthenogenesis?... geiger counter... The Muppets... er...

Paxman: This is embarrassing. *(Continued p. 94)*

(Continued p. 94)

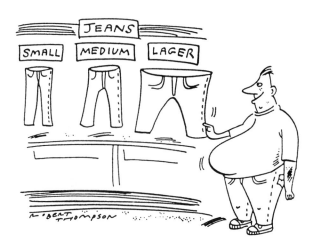

ST CAKES RAIDED IN DAWN PORN SWOOP

by Our Education Staff **Lunchtime O'Boys**

THE headmaster of St Cakes, the £6,000-a-term public school in the Midlands, was last night helping the police with their enquiries following the arrest of his entire staff and the seizure of the contents of the St Cakes school library.

The raid on St Cakes followed a complaint by parents about the school magazine, *The Cakeian*. The magazine usually carries reports of inter-house football matches, poems by sixth formers about the environment and reviews of the recent production of *Oliver*. However, in the current issue (Quinquasexima Term), the contents include photographs of the naked Geography Master (Mr C.D. "Grubby" Website) with members of the Remove in the showers.

Mr R.J. Kipling, speaking through his solicitors (Messrs Ben, Down and Smart) insisted that the school had nothing to hide.

"St Cakes has a long and proud tradition of paedophilia and it is one of the reasons why parents send their children here. It is all in the prospectus*."

Meanwhile, in his absence, the 14th century single-sex independent boys school (founded 1924) is being temporarily run by Mr G. Glitter (O.C.) who has stepped in at short notice.

The school is determined to continue as normal and has issued the following notices:

Fumblings will be run over the Upper Bottom on Dec 12th.

Trousers will come down on Dec 22nd (St Bandit's Day).

The service of Nine Lessons and Carols will be held in "C" Block of the Esther Rantzen Children's Home due to the choir having been taken into care.

28-page full-colour prospectus is available from the Bursar (Prisoner 7472412, 'A' Wing, Wormwood Scrubs)

'GOOD APPLES IN FORCE'
Knacker's shock claim

by Our Crime Staff **Nicked Ross**

"**I**T is the same in any organisation," said Inspector Knacker at a Scotland Yard press conference yesterday. "There are always a few people who insist on playing it by the book and doing their duty. But rest assured, gentlemen, we shall stop at nothing to root out these officers. There is no place for them in the modern police force."

The Inspector concluded: "I am now going to retire due to ill health and devote my life to bungee jumping for charity".

The Inspector is due to become Head of Security at Harrods for an annual salary of 500,000 copies of Punch (*surely 'pounds'? Ed.*).

"I'm experimenting with surrealist Cubism!"

25

THE EYE SALUTES THE PEOPLE'S QUEEN — 50 GLORIOUS YEARS

Spare a million quid, lady?

One doesn't carry small change

———— ☆ ————

I'll have a large gin and tonic, please, steward

———— ☆ ————

Long Live our Noble Queen….

That's the idea, son

QUEEN MEETS BLAIR AT PEOPLE'S BANQUET

That People's Menu in full

Person-Size Prawns in Garlic

— ✳ —

Life Baron of Beef

— ✳ —

Mr Edward Potatoes, Baked Not In Their Dinner-Jackets

— ✳ —

Commoner of Puddings

— ✳ —

To drink:

Vin Ordinary Working-Class People
followed by
Monsieur Napoleon Brandy

The Queen will propose the Loyal Toast to Mr Blair. After this, no one may smoke except Mr Ecclestone.

"Have you let the cat watch Tom and Jerry again?"

Restoration of Windsors a triumph

by Our Architectural Staff Sir Gawaine Commemorative Stamp

ONLY two months ago it seemed that the Windsors had been damaged beyond repair.

They had been reduced to a smoking ruin, covered with a thick film of filth and sleaze and blackened by every hack in Fleet Street.

But today, incredible as it seems, they have been lovingly restored to their former glory by a team of Britain's finest craftsmen.

Brown Nose Windsor Soup

Working round the clock, with the traditional materials of newspaper articles and television reports, these experts have utterly transformed the Windsors into a stunning replica of a popular monarchy.

● *The Queen and the Duke of Edinburgh have been regilded as a devoted couple who have stuck together for 50 years.*

● *Prince Charles has undergone extensive refurbishment to make him safe to the public.*

● *The Queen Mother, who had avoided the worst of the damage, has now been dusted down and brought out to save the life of a toddler.*

When the new-look House of Windsor was unveiled today, critics gasped with admiration and cried: "God Save Our Gracious Press! We know how to sell newspapers".

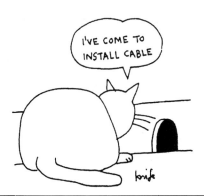

I'VE COME TO INSTALL CABLE

Pick Of The Season's Films

Family Choice

Holiday Friday 9.00am, BBC1

Reservoir Dwarves (1996)
Tarantino's brilliant homage to *Snow White and the Seven Dwarves*. Whoopi Goldberg is Snow White with Arnold Schwarzenegger, Sly Stallone, Jean Claude van Damme, Gene Hackman, Joe Pesci, Bruce Willis and John Travolta as the dwarves. Exciting climax to the action with a heavy-duty dwarf shoot-out in the witch's penthouse suite in Manhattan. *(125 minutes)*

Kiddies' Favourite

New Year's Eve Day
2.00pm, Channel 5

Shoot His Brains Out (1964)
Little-seen Clint Eastwood vehicle set in the Mexican borderlands. Clint is the mysterious drifter El Tel who kills 523 people before the titles. Score by Ernio Morcambandwiso. *(79 minutes)*

Children's Classic

New Year's Day Morning
7.00am, Channel 4

Bongo! (1969)
Michael Caine stars as Lieutenant Alan Clark of the Queen's Own Philanderers sent to quell the Bongo uprising in 1875. Star studded cast includes Wilfred Hyde White as Chief Bongolezi, leader of the legendary Bongo Warrior Tribe; Barbara Windsor as Queen Victoria; and Jim Dale as Disraeli. *(228 minutes)*

Best Of The Bunch

New Year's Day Evening
7.00pm, Carlton

They Flew To Bruges (1997)
Explosive Kung-Fu version of the British wartime classic originally starring David Tomlinson as Group Captain "Chalky" Sebag-Montefiore and Richard Attenborough as Gunner Wapshot. Directed by Fah-Kee Tup, the legendary martial arts master from Hong Kong, this version has the RAF mission to Bruges recast as a drugs delivery to Shanghai. Stars No-Too Good, Ho Plez, and Tun-Eee Toff. *(398 minutes)*

(That's enough terrible films. Ed.)

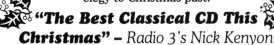

UPFRONTERS

GOES TO DOWNING STREET!

It's the ultimate celebrity do — New Year at No. 10!

1 She's the **Cherie** on the cake! No wonder **Gerald** thinks he's a lucky **Kaufman**! As they say — **Blair** today, gone to the Opera House tomorrow! Still, what a great Labour Party! *(You're fired. Ed.)*

2 It's a Man Behaving Badly! That's a **Clune** as to who is kissing the mystery blonde! Got the answer yet? **Ulrika**! It's our **Martin** making Ms **Jonsson** see Shooting Stars! *(This is really feeble. You're rehired. Ed.)* Who cares? The main thing is that it's a great Labour Party!

3 It's Virgin on the ridiculous! They've brought out the **Branson** again but **Richard**'s not complaining! Not when he's taking **Denise van Outen** herself! That's Big Breakfast of him! Hang on a minute — it might be **Jeremy Irons** and **Helen Mirren**! Or is it **Rory McGrath** with **Kirsty Young** from Channel Five News? Perhaps it's **Sean Bean** with **Zoe Ball**? Anyway, whoever they are, there's no denying that this is a great Labour Party! *(This is pathetic. You're fired. Ed.)*

4 United again! **David** is obviously at the lady's **Beckham** call! But she's no **Posh**-over and he'll have to make some Spice between the posts if he is to score! *(You're fired again — and don't use the Labour Party joke to finish. Ed.)* Happy New Year — and what a great Labour Party this is!!

The Alternative Rocky Horror Service Book

No. 94: Service to be performed by the Archbishop of Canterbury in Asda over the period of Christmas and the Epiphany.

Carey: O Lord, open thou our doors.

All: And our mouths shall start watering with all the delicious things on display.

Carey: The first shall be last and the last first

All: Not in here, mate. Out the way. That's my trolley.

The Address

Carey: I welcome you all here to Asda — and did not the three wise men see "A Sda" shining in the East? *(Here the congregation may laugh or not).* Today is a very important one for us all here. I bring good news and glad tidings of great joy. There are seasonal offers on all the following items:

The Reading

Carey: Low Fat Shepherd's Pie: Was £1.30: Now £1.29. Angel Delight, banana flavour: Was £59p: Now £58p. Packet of 200 Camel Cigarettes: Was £29.99: Now £30.00

The Blessing

Carey: Frozen Peas be with you.

All: And with thy spirits and alcoholic beverages — particularly the Drambuie which is 6p off. *(The choir and congregation will now sing "The Trolley and the Ivy" (Trad) or similar piece of seasonal muzak)*

Carey: Let us pay. *(The congregation shall now process to the checkout points excepting those with "8 sins or less" who may go directly to a special till where they shall be ministered unto by Sheryl and Dean — or it may be Dawn and Darren)*

All: The Lord be with you.

Carey: And Wayne also if you require assistance bagging up your purchases.

All: Asdamen.

PICK OF THE PANTOS

"Newt in Boots"

The People's National
Theatre, Brent

TV's Ken Livingstone plays the young man who wants to become Mayor of London. With his pet newt, Trotsky, Ken sets off to see if the streets are properly paved or if they need alternative access facilities for the disabled.

But the evil Lord Archer (played by TV's Jeffrey Archole) has other plans. He wants to be Lord Mayor of London himself and thus become really powerful and famous.

Merry mayhem ensues when Chinese launderer Mr

Wishy-Washy (played by TV's Chris Patten) intervenes saying that *he* wants the job as well.

And if that wasn't enough,

the wicked Genie of the Lamp (played by Peter Mandelson of TV fame) decides that Ken and his newt will *never* be in charge of London!

Hilarious songs, dances, sketches and jokes aplenty!

Watch out, Lord Archer, nobody's behind you.

Oh yes they are!

Oh no they are not!

You're right. They're not...

WHAT THEY SAID

"A terrific romp,"
– The Daily Star

"We apologise to Lord Archer for suggesting that he was in any way involved in a romp of any nature,"
– The Daily Star

"What would you like us to say about it, Mr Campbell?"
– The Mirror

New game for parents

IN THE COURTS

Clark vs Hastings and the Evening Standard (Day 94)

THE CASE continued today in front of Mr Justice Cocklecarrot in which Rt Hon Alan Clark seeks to restrain himself from groping Mrs Edith Musgrove, 56, a court usher from Ealing *(surely 'restrain the Evening Standard from publishing a spoof account of his groping Mrs Edith Musgrove' Ed).*

Sir Ephraim Cucumber Q.C. *(for Mr Clark)*: What were your feelings, Mr Clark, when you read this appalling parody of yourself in the Evening Standard dated July 7th, 1997? *(Holds up copy of Playboy)* I am sorry, your Honour, I appear to have the wrong bundle.

Cocklecarrot: It looks like a right bundle of fun to me, Sir Ephraim!

(Loud sycophantic laughter from barristers greets judge's feeble joke)

Sir Ephraim *(reading)*: "Terrific lunch. Got rather squiffy and made an arse of myself in the Commons. Made a pass at Betty Boothroyd (no luck) and did Hitler impersonation behind Major's back. Crashed Porsche doing 200mph down

Lord North Street. Still, bit of luck in the hospital. Cracking dusky nurse from Bongo-Bongo land with tits the size of the Matterhorn. Blimey!"

(Laughter and cheers of "Good old Clarkie" fill court)

Clark: When I read this I of course thought I had written it. So did my friends and they all rang up to congratulate me on such a wonderfully funny piece.

Cucumber: No, no, no, Mr Clark. You're supposed to say that you were very upset and distressed to see yourself portrayed as a sex-crazed fascist drunk and loony.

Clark: Sorry. I had a bit of a heavy lunch with this cracking totty I met on the tube.

Cucumber *(hurriedly)*: No further questions.

Clark: I've got one. Has the judge got a wife and daughters? I've got nothing on this evening, or I won't have with a bit of luck.

(The Nutcase continues)

"Eric's gone 'off-message' "

I promise to love, honour and obey Mrs Thatcher

Trevor McDonald's Anthology

ONE of my favourite poems, just in, describes the fate of a grandiose building project, erected by a megalomaniac. **Percy Bysshe Shelley** has that story.

OZYMANDELSON

I met a traveller from an antique land
Who said: "One vast and trunkless plastic dome
Stands in the desert. Near it on the sand,
Half sunk, a shattered visage lies, whose frown
And wrinkled lip and sneer of cold command
Tell that its sculptor well those passions read
Which yet survive, stamped on these lifeless things,
The hand that mocked them and the heart that fed.
And on the pedestal these words appear:
"My name is Ozymandelson, King of Kings:
Look on my work, ye mighty, and have a good laugh!"
Nothing beside remains. Round the decay
Of that colossal wreck, boundless and bare,
The lone and level marshes stretch far away.

LEONARDO OUTED SHOCK

by Our Art Staff **Genda Slagg and Lunchtime O'Boys**

THE GAY world was rocked to its foundations yesterday when it was discovered that the most celebrated homosexual artist in history, Leonardo da Vinci, was not after all gay but a secret and sordid heterosexual, who got his kicks from makng love to women.

The disclosures come from a series of hitherto suppressed invoices addressed to the artist from Signora Tutti-Frutti, proprietor of Il Bordello di Milano.

Typical was one bill which read as follows:

Feast Of The Immaculate Conception, Yeare of Our Lorde Fourteen Hundred And Ninety-Two

To: Signor da Vinci

For: Services Rendered by

Signorina Mona di
Lisa . . . . 5 Gold Ducats
(window tax not included)

under which the artist had written, "Paid with thanks. See you Wednesday. Keep smiling!"

Said a spokesman for the Gay and Lesbian Rights pressure group, Outrage: "Clearly this bill is a total forgery, drummed up by the straight Establishment in a desperate bid to reclaim the foremost gay icon of all time for their own, which he is not and never will be."

NEW LABOUR, NEW DISNEY

Hi Ho! Hi Ho! It's off welfare and to work we go...

MICKEY SAYS NO TO MANDY MEETING

by Our Man in Florida
Lunchtime O'Rlando

MR Michael Mouse, the well-known Disney spokesman, yesterday created a storm when he refused to be photographed shaking hands with the cartoon character Mandy Mandelson.

"I am a serious figure," said Mr Mouse, "and I cannot afford to ruin my reputation by association with an internationally recognised joke figure."

Mr Mouse continued: "Mandy has a silly voice and funny ears and you won't catch me making a fool of myself with him for the cameras".

Humphrey the cat is 79.

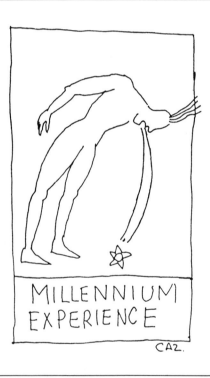

MILLENNIUM EXPERIENCE

CAZ.

"Why must they drag religion in to it?"

PARKY'S BACK!

by Our TV Staff **Christina "Lunchtime" O'Done**

IT WAS just like the old days.

From the wings a familiar, grey-haired figure bounced onto the stage to a hail of applause.

The chat-up king was back, ready to entertain the nation and to prove that the young kids had nothing on old Parky.

"Will you give a warm welcome," he said, "to my very good friend — someone who needs no introduction — or rather he does, because no one knows who he is — Bill Hague!"

That was how the veteran Tory chairman launched his come-back, after years in the wilderness.

Said one critic, Sara Keays: "There's no one to match Parky for the quality of his questions. Ranging from 'What are you doing later?' to 'Would you like to be my researcher?', they combine the qualities of *(cont'd p.94)*

EVERY PARENT'S WORST NIGHTMARE

by Glenda Lee-Potsmoker OBE

IT IS every parent's worst nightmare.

You never think that it will happen to you.

But then one day you wake up to find that your own daughter has become a journalist on the Daily Mirror.

Nothing can prepare you for the shock that this news will bring.

One minute she is a lovely little girl, playing innocently in the garden with her Barbie dolls.

The next she is hanging about in seedy pubs trying to entrap the Home Secretary's son and shop him to the police as a drug dealer.

DAWN RAID

There are no words to describe the heartache which follows the sickening realisation that your beloved little teenage toddler is now a blonde slapper mixing with some of the most degraded elements in modern society, viz the staff of the Daily Mirror.

"It is every parents' worst nightmare," said Mrs Ludmilla Alford, when she refused to speak to us yesterday at her luxury, 2-bedroom Sunbury home about her daughter Dawn, whom we cannot name for legal reasons.

"We did everything for her," her father might have added, had either of Dawn's parents been prepared to talk to us.

"She had a first-class education, her school reports were always glowing, she had lots of friends and she was popular with staff and students alike.

DOPE

"But now she hangs around with some of the most notorious pushers in London — men like Piers 'The Moron' Moron and Dave 'The Fool Monty' Montgomery.

"These heartless men have made a fortune out of other people's suffering by exploiting the gullible public's addiction to 'shit', as it is called.

"And now," Mr Alford might have concluded, "we have lost our little girl to the twilight world of the Daily Mirror."

Make no mistake. This is the nightmare that every parent dreads.

(You've done this bit. Ed.)

"Does he talk?"

HOUSE OF COMMONS
OFFICIAL REPORT

PARLIAMENTARY DEBATES

Han-z-z-zard

3.00 Prime Minister's Question Time

Ms Patsy Jacket *(Tunbridge Wells, New Lab)*: Would the Prime Minister agree that our party is very keen on single mothers and will do everything it can to create more of them, which is exactly what my Rt Honourable friend the Foreign Secretary has done by so bravely leaving his wife?

Mr Tony Blair *(Sedgemore, New Lab)*: Thank you for asking that, Patsy. You read it out very well. I'll give you another question next week. *(Labour cheers, cries of "Give us a job!")*

Mr John Madcow *(Sleazegone, New Con)*: May I say how very nice it is to see the Prime Minister back in the House for a change?

Mr Tony Blair: Look, I didn't come all this way from Japan just to be patronised by a member of the party opposite which made such an appalling mess of this country over the last 18 years. But now, thanks to the policies we've inherited, we have the strongest economy in Europe. I hope that will help the honourable member to keep his cakehole firmly closed in future. *(Labour cheers, cries of "Good old Tony!")*

Mr William Squitt *(Woebegone, New Con)*: Would the Prime Minister like to tell the House whether the taxpayers of this country are expected to pay for his Rt Hon Friend the Foreign Secretary's new bit of fluff to traipse around the world with him?

Tony Blair: I refer the Rt Hon member to the holiday I took a few moments ago.

Mr Paddy Ashtray *(Pantsdown, Old Lib Dem)*: Can I ask my honourable friend the Prime Minister whether he remembers who I am?

(MPs leave chamber en masse for important briefing sessions with their researchers)

RICHARD LOVES TO SURF THE NET TO EXCHANGE IDEAS WITH LIKE MINDED PEOPLE AROUND THE WORLD

BESTIE

10 TELLTALE SIGNS THAT YOUR DAUGHTER MIGHT BE A DAILY MIRROR REPORTER

1. Looks shifty and withdrawn.

2. Refuses to say what she's up to.

3. Bedroom begins to fill with suspicious "equipment", such as tape-recorders, microphones, etc.

4. Finds it difficult to use long words.

5. Can no longer tell the difference between truth and fiction.

6. Suddenly becomes very rich for no obvious reason.

7. Er…

8. …that's it.

That Mo Mowlam Breakthrough Peace Plan In Full

1. New "power-sharing" 78-seat consultative assembly to sit at Stormont on alternate Tuesdays. With responsibility for tourism, the environment and cheese.

2. A grand Council of the Isles with representatives from Scotland, Wales, Jersey, Rockall, Malin, Fastnet, Finistere, Fredastaire and Norway (nul points).

3. New Cross-Border Peacekeeping Force, made up equally of former members of the INLA, the UVF, the UDI, the IRA and the PVC to ensure continuing violence and to promote tourism.

4. A number of Hollywood films to be made every year on location in Ireland and Ulster, starring Bruce Willis, Mickey Rourke or Liam Neeson as lovable ex-terrorists who work tirelessly for peace by shooting each other.

5. Direct rule by British Government.

6. United Ireland at once.

7. Er…

8. That's it.

Sunday Telegraph

How I Went Up In An Aeroplane

by Dominic Lawson (aged 40)

THE most exciting thing I did on my holidays was to go up in an aeroplane. It was a Harrier jump jet like they have in wars on TV! It was great and I wasn't even sick like my friend Max Hastings was!

Before it took off I was very frightened. But the pilot said, "Don't worry, son, this will make a good column for the Sunday Telegraph."

©World Copyright Ministry of Defence

"Fire away"

NORTHERN IRELAND TALKS

THE ULSTER PUZZLER

1. The Amazing Maze!

Can you find your way through the Maze and kill another prisoner? Careful you don't take a wrong turning — and watch out for all the security guards! *(Difficulty rating: Nil)*

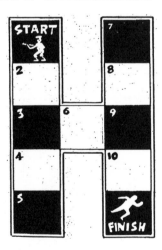

START 7 2 8 3 6 9 4 10 5 FINISH

2. Brain Teaser

Why is the Maze called a High Security Prison?
Answer: Sorry. The answer escapes me! (Geddit?)

3. Search Me!

Can you find the hidden item in the block? The prison officers can't!
(That's enough puzzles. Ed)

A B C
G U N
D E F

St Cakes

Internet Term begins today. There are 3000 computers in the school. A.J.P. Webcrawler (Browsers) is Keeper of the Mouse. E.E.E. Mail (Messages) is Senior Menu Bar. Mr R.P.D. Double-Click (Head of Information Technology) has replaced all other members of staff. Screensavers will be held on All Anoraks' Day, 4th March. On 31st March there will be a downloading from http://www.hotdaneporn.com of *Dutch Dental Assistants Go Bonking Mad*, directed by Simon Cyber-Filth (O.C.). There will be a service of deconsecration of the school chapel on Easter Saturday before it is refurbished as a sixth form Internet Cafe. Shutdowns will be on 7th April.

"Psst, Señor! Feelthy websites?"

New Naval Sea Shanties

'Twas on the good ship HMS Venus
My God you should have seen us,
The officer was extremely good at his job,
But made some unfortunate remarks to
A Wren which were taken out of context.
(Case closed)

CHERIE SHOCK

And what do you do?

Telepubbies

Drinky Winky.

Tipsy.

Laa-Laa.

Po.

Opera News
New Season at Garsington

Il Trionfo di Leonardo

FIRST-ever performance of long-lost Haydn opera about an 18th Century landowner Don Leonardo Ingrami who entertains his rich friends by staging agreeable musical masques and pageants in the exquisite gardens of his country mansion. But the local peasantry, led by the formidable Donna Mobile, are enraged by the harmless noise of aristocratic revelry. In protest they sing the now-famous Strimmers' Chorus, accompanied by the sound of lawn mowers, klaxons and motor horns.

One particularly imaginative villager flies over the stage in one of M. Montgolfier's early hot-air balloons, carrying the legend "Hoot if you hate Haydn". Act Two begins with Don Ingrami being arrested for the crime of "noise pollution" by officers of the South Oxfordshire District Council. He is put on trial and in his defence sings the beautiful aria "Buon giorno magistrato", in which he suggests to the judge that, since he is clearly a very civilised fellow, he might like to bring his wife to a future performance, with front row seats and a champagne supper to follow. The judge sees the strength of Don Ingrami's legal arguments, and orders that the riotous peasantry should be put to death.

Initially Signore Vivaldi toyed with a fifth seasonal concerto...

'LA PRIMAVERA'   'L'ESTATE'   'LA SILLEE'   'L'AUTUMN'   'L'INVERNO'

Lookalikes

Ideal Home model **Peter Mandelson**

Monica **Barbie**

Sir,
Has anyone noticed the close resemblance of new "Barrister" Barbie to her sister in arms and all American legal eagle, Clinton aide, Monica Lewinsky (24)? The fresh "I can't believe it's not butter wouldn't melt in my mouth" look is most inspiring.

Sincerely,
L. WHITE,

London E3.

Scream **Trophy**

Sir,
I wonder whether any of your readers have noticed, as my family has, the uncanny resemblance between Munch's painting "The Scream" and the Football World Cup trophy as depicted in THE GUARDIAN recently. Could they by any chance be related? I think we should be told.

Yours sincerely,
MARTIN CLARE,

Fairford, Glos.

Sir,
Surely I am not the only one to notice the remarkable resemblance between Westminster icon Peter Mandelson and the Ideal Home catalogue model for Snore No More. Moonlighting perhaps?

Yours faithfully,
VERONICA HITCHCOCK,

London SW1.

BBC **Babel**

Sir,
I wonder if any of your readers have noticed the similarity between the BBC (Nation shall speak peace unto Nation) and the Tower of Babel (Nation shall speak gibberish unto Nation)?

Yours sincerely,
DAVID ROBSON,

Leeds.

Deedes **Weeto**

Sir,
It's a shame that a great reporter, distinguished editor and former MP should be reduced to promoting breakfast cereal. Couldn't Lord Copper and Lord Gnome get together charitably so W.H. Deedes didn't have to impersonate Professor Weeto to earn a crust?

Yours etc,
NICK RANKING,

London WC2.

Ronnie **Cherie**

Sir,
I wonder whether any of your readers have noticed the extraordinary resemblance between Ronnie Wood who plays with new Britpop sensation The Rolling Stones, and Cherie Blair who plays with new Britpop sensation Tony Blair.

Yours Marianne faithfully,
PAUL DOMENET,

Plaistow, W. Sussex.

Cook **Père Tanguy**

Sir,
I wonder if any readers could explain the curious resemblance between Van Gogh's Père Tanguy and our illustrious legover foreign secretary, Robin Cook?

Cheers,
C. CAREY,

Address unknown.

Boss **New Boss**

I couldn't help noticing a disconcerting resemblance between the recently deposed leader of Indonesia, President Suharto, and his pro-democracy replacement Mr Habibie. It is presumably fortunate for the people of Indonesia that they are not related.

Yours truly,
S.M. FOX,

London N4.

Camille **Dot**

Sir,
I couldn't help noticing the similarity between this famous opinion-former Dot Cotton of EastEnders and Camille Paglia. Could they, by any chance, be related?

Yours faithfully,
K.F. JOHN,
London SE21.

Before **After**

Sir,
Something fishy's going on at Birds Eye. Here is Cap'n Birds Eye as we all know him. But now look... Is he on Viagra? Or is it something in the fish fingers? I think we should be told.

Yours sincerely,
PENNY WAINWRIGHT,

Rawdon, Leeds.

Gazza   **Jefferson**

Sir,

Has anyone noticed the uncanny resemblance between Paul Gascoigne and Thomas Jefferson, the one-time American president?

Whilst Paul, or "Gazza" as he is familiarly known, has shown the world an admirable example of tireless dedication to the good of his country, Jefferson was known to be the epitome of the irresponsible lout who sets a very poor image of his countrymen abroad with foul gestures to the press and even acts of violence to his young bride for which he needed therapy.

Yours etc,
MICHAEL CLARK,
Tewin, Herts.

ernard   **Mother**

These pictures were on facing pages of today's ESTERN MORNING NEWS. With such parallel es and coincidental deaths, do you think they ht be related?

Yours,
NIGEL AYERS,
nwall.

Vita

I wonder whether any of your readers have ced the extraordinary resemblance between while Dr Who, Tom Baker, and notorious writer Sackville-West. His recent autobiography is ously silent on their relationship.

Yours faithfully,
ROBERT BENNETT,
stead, Surrey.

Straw   **Demon**

Sir,

Has anybody noticed the startling resemblance between scourge of all drug dealers Mr Jack Straw and that scourge of all children the Demon Headmaster? Are possibly both their campaigns to be despotic rulers of all they survey related? I think the Education Secretary should be told!

MARK HUNTER,
Via e-mail.

Sir,

While browsing through a Littlewoods' mail-order catalogue the other day, I came across an almost-identical version of the celebrated £2,000 dress worn by Ms Ffion Jenkins at a Tory Conference cocktail party. The catalogue dress is priced at £35.

Does the Tory leader share his future wife's lavish shopping habits? I think we should be told.

ANNIE GELLY,
London SE24.

Winnie   **Elton**

Sir,

I wonder whether any of your readers have noticed the striking resemblance between Winnie Mandela and the popular pianist, Elton John, as I have?

Both are mad about football teams and jewellery, so I am sure they must be related in some way.

Yours faithfully,
WILL HAVERCROFT,
Oxford.

Madame Moitessier   **Bragg**

Sir,

Can there be French blood in the veins of Melvyn Bragg?

Yours faithfully,
MRS E. HEWISON,
London SW20.

Smithers   **Smith**

Sir,

Have any of your other readers noticed the uncanny resemblance between Waylon Smithers from THE SIMPSONS — loyal servant to an evil, power crazed boss whom he secretly fancies — and Chris Smith, Culture Tzar?

Yours faithfully,
JAMES OLIVER,
Bury St Edmunds, Suffolk.

Rembrandt   **Whitehouse**

Sir,

On a recent visit to Amsterdam I was struck by this portrait of Rembrandt saying "Suit you, sir" in 17th-century Dutch. Apparently a descendant of his, called Paul Whitehouse, is currently resident in England.

Yours sincerely,
BEDE ROGERSON,
East Dereham, Norfolk.

Gordon Brown   **"Boy Bitten by a Lizard"**

Sir,

Is this Caravaggio painting of a lookalike Gordon Brown allegorical? I think we should be told.

GED HOBAN,
Christchurch, Dorset.

Apology

IN COMMON with all other newspapers, we may in recent years have given the impression that the economies of the Asian nations were in some way the most successful in the world. Headlines such as "Up, Up And Away — Malaysian Growth Hits 80 Per Cent", "Korean Dragon Is World Beater" and "Put A Tiger In Your Bank — How Pacific Rim Countries Have Solved Riddle Of Eternal Wealth" might have conveyed the notion that we regarded the Far Eastern economies as a model for the future which we poor Westeners could only view with helpless envy.

We now recognise that there was not a jot or scintilla of truth in any of the above. The so-called "tiger economies" are, we now realise, deeply corrupt, inefficient oligarchies, run on slave labour, and wholly dependent on the billions of dollars they have shamelessly borrowed from Western banks, and which they are now in no position to repay. We are very sorry if our earlier reports led to any confusion in the minds of our readers or caused them to invest their money in these worthless "junk economies". We would like to suggest to them that they should know better than to believe anything they read in newspapers.

"Buy swords"

'CARE IN THE COMMUNITY TO BE SCRAPPED' says Blair

by TV Psychiatrist **Dr Chaj Perhour**

THE Government has announced an end to the controversial "care in the community" scheme which, according to the Prime Minister, has allowed "people with unfortunate psychological flaws to be let out onto the streets of London, particularly Downing Street".

Mr Blair cited the sad example of a Gordon B who, despite clear mental instability, was permitted to endanger innocent members of the public like himself with vicious and unprovoked attacks brought on by delusions of grandeur.

Said Mr Blair: "The man was obviously bonkers, talked gibberish to any biographer who would listen and most ludicrous of all actually believed that he was the Prime Minister.

"This man should be locked up in a secure institution such as the Treasury and should never be heard of again."

Tales of Merrie England

The Legend Of Robin Cook And His Merry Women

NOW in the England of those days there was no man more hated than Bad King John, a weak tyrant who held the nation in his thrall.

The only men who dared oppose him were a band of brave outlaws, living in the shadowy depths of Walworth Road.

And none of that band was as red of beard and bright of eye as Robin the Cook.

Robin was more feared by John's men than any other in that brave group of outlaws — yea, more so even than Little John Prescott, Friar Dobson or the beautiful Maid Mandelson.

And he was best known for his long bow and his prowess in the ancient sport of legover.

Wherever he appeared, both young and old would gather round to greet him with this happy song:

Robin Cook, Robin Cook,
With his beard so red.
Robin Cook, Robin Cook,
Getting into bed.
Loved by his secretary, hated by
*   his wife,*
Robin Cook, Robin Cook,
Robin Cook...

Indeed, as they roamed the countryside, promising to rob the rich and give to the poor, Robin's fame grew apace.

But at last the day came when weak King John was driven from his home by a terrible landslide.

Then Good King Tony was restored to rule wisely over the good folk of England, and he made Robin the chiefest of his counsellors.

But the people's rejoicing did not last e'en a nine-month.

For King Tony's first edict was that his men should go out to rob the poor in order to give to the rich.

And his second edict was that brave Robin should henceforth travel alone on the King's business and not take any of his Merrie Women with him — particularly not Mistress Gaynor.

And the people began sadly to sing a new song:

Robin Cook, Robin Cook,
With his beard so red.
Robin Cook, Robin Cook,
All alone in bed.
Loved by the press, hated by
*   the rest,*
Robin Cook, brought to book,
Robin Cook.

NEXT WEEK: King Tony the Lionheart changes his mind and lets Mistress Gaynor travel with Willy Scarlet (surely 'Robin Cook'? Ed.)

LIFE CYCLE

THOSE CHRISTIAN DOME EXPERIENCES IN FULL

What you will see in the year 2000

1. Puppet show of complete Old Testament with Sooty as Moses, Sweep as Solomon, and Basil Brush as the prophet Ezekiel (Boom! Boom!) *(10am Stall 194)*

2. The Last Supper On Ice — Torvill and Dean recreate the final Passover Meal with music by Chris de Burgh. *(11.30am The Mandelson Hall)*

3. The Virtual Book of Revelations — state-of-the-art laser video game where *you* are the Beast, the Antichrist bringing darkness to the world. *(Stall No 666)*

4. The Feeding of the Five Thousand Snack Bar. Try our Filet-o-Fish with a sesame seed bap! It's divine! *(All main thoroughfares)*

5. Pontius Pilate Go Kart Ride — details to be announced.

(That's enough christianity. Ed.)

THE XANADULY TELEGRAPH

OPPOSITION TO PLEASURE DOME MOUNTS

by Nicholas Taylor Coleridge

Public opinion is hardening against plans by Kubla Khandelson to build an ancient pleasure dome on a site in Xanadu.

"The project is a fiasco," say critics. "Khandelson is a dictator who expects everyone to do whatever he decrees. The twice--five--mile--round, wall--and--tower--girdled site near the River Alph is very difficult for people to visit — and moreover there are no ideas as to how to fill up the caverns measureless to man."

Kubla Khandelson denied this, saying that he had just returned from a trip to Opium World where *(not continued due to Mr Coleridge's failure to complete this report)*

'NO ROOM FOR CONRAN IN HEAVEN,' says God

by Our Millennium Staff **Sara Fim and Cherry Bim**

THE Celestial City was rocked to its foundations today by reports that there would be no room in the "Dome of Heaven" for Sir Terence Conran, the distinguished designer of sofas.

Sources close to God were alleged to have told the world's media that "the Almighty considers it inappropriate to allow in a devout atheist, just because Mr Blair goes to his restaurant".

But in a clarification statement issued later by spin angels, a heavenly spokesman said: "The Almighty has been misquoted, as so often before.

Sofa No Good

"Heaven is a multi-faith society with room for all shades of belief or none.

"We up here will certainly recognise the part played by Sir Terence in supplying stripped pine duvets for young couples in the Seventies.

The Son of God is roughly 2000.

'SAVE BALDY'S MEDALS' — WIFE'S TEARFUL PLEA

by **E.I. Erewego**, Our Man At The Francis Bacon Exhibition At The Hayward Gallery *(shome mishtake surely? Ed.)*

THE SOCCER world was rocked to its foundations yesterday by the news that Marilyn Pevsner, 68, estranged wife of Neasden FC's own-goal wizard "Baldy" Pevsner, is to sell her husband's priceless collection of soccer memorabilia.

"I am gutted that I have to do this," she told newsmen yesterday, "but financial circumstances leave me no alternative. I now call upon the Government to step in and save the collection for the nation."

Moore Means More

Reporters were yesterday given a glimpse of what Marilyn described as "Neasden's Crown Jewels".

Taking the lid off an old shoebox she revealed:

● Commemorative set of medals of 1966 World Cup, mounted on simulated velvet with legend "With the compliments of Lex Garages, Wembley Road. Score every time with Lex. Manager: P. Middleton Davis" (Nobby Stiles and Geoff Hurst missing)

● Collection of cups dated 1973-1979 commemorating various North Circular tournaments with assorted legends, including "Nice one Baldy", "Sack Ron Knee" and "Ooh-ah Wally Foot!"

A Sotheby's spokesman yesterday described the Pevsner collection as "literally priceless".

"I wouldn't pay any price for it whatsoever," he said.

LATE SCORE

North Circular Relegation League

Manchester United 0
Neasden 0

MAN OF MATCH: Neasden's exciting No. 4 shirt ex-President Mobutu of Zaire

Brian Sewell hails a taxi

THE CORRECT ANSWER

Raising standards in
education

Mr Byers — what is 8 times 7?

It's too early to say… you can't expect me to put a figure on it… it's under review

TEACHERS STUNNED BY BLUNKETT'S SHOCK PLAN

by Our Schools Staff **Lunchtime O'Level**

THE WORLD of education reacted in disbelief last night at the revolutionary plan put forward by Mr David Blunkett to raise standards in Britain's primary schools.

Teaching unions went on strike, school governors resigned en masse and local education authorities threatened to shut down thousands of school when Mr Blunkett unveiled his dramatic 3-point blueprint:

1. Pupils should be taught to read.
2. Pupils should be taught to write.
3. Pupils should be taught how to count up to 10.

THE **ALTERNATIVE VOICE**

Dave Spart, Co-Chair of the Bermondsey Primary School Assistants Against Iraqi Sanctions Alliance.

Er... it is utterly sickening to see the so-called Education Secretary telling teachers that they are failing pupils when we all know that the concept of failure and success in education is totally outdated and discredited and merely encourages social divisiveness, class factionalism and er basically fascism whereas we the working members of the teaching profession currently on strike should be judged performance-wise only on a continual assessment basis by our own professional peers, i.e. other teachers, rather than inspected in an artificially constructed judgemental environment, i.e. the current quasi-examination situation blatantly designed to weed out those who cannot teach er *(Cont. page 94)*

PARLIAMENTARY DEBATES
Han-z-z-zard

3.15: President Blair's Question Time

Mr William Squitt *(Woebegone, Con)*: Could the Prime Minister explain why the taxpayers should have to pay for a new double bed for the Foreign Secretary's official residence, at a cost of £129.99? *(Tory cheers, cries of "Cooky Nooky!", "Resign!", etc)*

Mr Tony Blair *(Sedgemore, New Lab)*: I find it completely pathetic that the Rt Hon Gentleman should ask such a pathetic question. It just shows how pathetic he is, asking such a pathetic question.

(Labour cheers, cries of "We love you, Tony!", "Can I have a job when you've sacked Robin Cook?", etc)

Mr Squitt: I repeat my question. Can the Rt Hon Prime Minister explain the new bed? Yes or no.

Mr Blair: Alright. Yes, your question is pathetic. No *(takes out briefing note)* the last Conservative government spent more money on beds in the years 1983-8 than we have ever spent. They also spent 83 percent more on wallpaper, 56 percent more on travel for spouses and partners and no less than 198 percent more on Cheese-and-Onion Pringles at government functions. *(Labour cheers, cries of "Tony for king!", "Can we have a job when you've sacked Geoff Robinson, Harriet Harman, etc!")* I repeat. The Rt Hon Gentleman's question is pathetic. Why does the opposition concentrate on all these trivia, and never ask about our policies?

Mr Squitt: Because they are the same as ours. *(Uproar in House)*

Mr P. Ashtray *(Pantsdown, Old Lib Dem)*: Does anyone remember when I was at the centre of a sex scandal with my secretary?

(House empties as MPs rush for secretaries. Surely 'exits'? Ed.)

LATE NEWS

CHILD NOT MURDERED, RAPED OR MOLESTED SHOCK

IN AN astonishing piece of news, it was announced last night that no British child under the age of 10 had been assaulted for nearly five minutes and *(cont. p 94)*.

…AND LEATHER PATCHES ON THE ELBOWS

'Superteacher' gets a costume

THRIBB BREAKS LONG SILENCE
Poetry World Stunned

by Our Poetry Staff
Tom Apaulin

THE distinguished poet E.J. Thribb has broken 30 days of self-imposed silence following the tragic break-up of his relationship with fellow teenage poet Sylvia Krin (16 ½).

Thribb has always refused to comment on the affair, despite claims by feminists that Thribb was personally to blame for Sylvia failing her mock A-Levels, having a "bit of a nervous breakdown" and going to stay with her auntie in Eastbourne.

Now he has produced a new sequence of 94 poems called "Happy Birthday" in which the poet chronicles their doomed relationship.

Here is the pivotal poem — now reproduced *only* in the *Eye*:

So. Farewell then
Sylvia.

Today I saw
A poster for
Benidorm.

And it reminded
Me of our
Holiday there.

It was very
Hot.
And you got
Burnt.

Flaming red
Raw. Blood.
Flesh sizzling.
Ow.

You said it
Was my fault

But it wasn't.

People get
Burnt.

Especially when
They are in
Love.

E.J. Thribb (17½)

©*The Times*

TOMORROW: 'Quarrel in the Duty Free' — another amazing poem by Britain's greatest-ever poet.

A Doctor writes
Hip Operations

AS a doctor I am often asked, "Can you churn out 1000 words on the Queen Mother's hip replacement?"

The simple answer is: "Yes, of course, as soon as I've finished the piece on Kate Winslett's weight problem."

What happens in these cases is that the doctor writes a very long article and then puts in a big medical diagram (*graphicus superfluus normalis*) to fill up the space. Thus a genuine article can be replaced by a false, manufactured one.

Of course, there may be side effects for the reader, such as drowsiness and nausea, but the operation is usually a great success for the doctor who can walk away with a lot of money within weeks.

If you are worried about filling your pages, please contact me at once.

© *A Doctor.*

WOMAN SUES CLINTON OVER SEX SCANDAL

An American woman who once met the President at a White House social function has sensationally claimed that "he did not have casual sex with me".

The woman claims the President made a number of asexual remarks to her, such as "What do you do then?" and "Where are you from?"

She is now suing him for loss of earnings, claiming over £1 million in chat show, newspaper, film and book fees.

(Reuter)

I'm going to go down in history

Starsky

von Tripp

Scoopawicz

Havitovsky

Bugloss

Rees-Moggsky

Who are they – the main players in the biggest scandal the world has ever known?

● United States Prosecutor **Hiram J. Starsky**. A remorseless investigator charged with probing the allegations of sexual impropriety made against President Clintstone by Paula Yatesky, 38, a Little Rock stenographer, who claims $10 billion compensation for "interpersonal sexualistic invasionment" by the President in an Arkansas motel room in 1971.

● **Maria von Tripp**. Former White House aide who agreed to act as agent provocateur for Starsky *(see above)*. Later she secretly taped conversations between herself and Monica Havitovsky, 21, *(see below)* who was sleeping with President Clintosterone as part of her work experience programme. She will be a key witness in any Congressional impeachment proceedings under Article 69 of the Constitution which forbids "acts of non-penetrative sexual oralisation between the President of the United States and any person or persons who are not his lawful wedded partner".

● **Sam Scoopawicz**, Chief Reporter of *Newsweek*, who bravely decided not to publish the Clintstone-Havitovsky tapes which had been passed to him by von Tripp *(see above)* at the instigation of prosecutor Starsky but instead leaked them in full on the Internet.

● **Monica Havitovsky**, 21, the White House intern who admitted to von Tripp (see above) in 90 hours of tape-recorded interviews that she had enjoyed "non-penetrative oral relationship sessions" with President Jefferson Clintoblerone whom she nicknamed "Gobbledygook". She has pleaded the Fifth Amendment through her lawyer Marvin Z. Toothbrush *(see below)* who is trying to win for his client immunity "from prosecution for perjury after she was subpoenaed in the Paula Yatesky hearings" (see above).

● **Sylvester Bugloss Jr**, 48. High-school teacher and former lover of Havitovsky *(see above)*, Bugloss now claims that Havitovsky was a "compulsive fantasist" who told his wife Zedka Bugloss that she was having an affair with her husband, which she was.

● **William Rees-Moggsky**, 98, ageing British columnist and former Editor of the Times whose articles on the Clintstone scandal are read by no one. *(That's enough key players in the greatest scandal of the century. Ed.)*

MEET THE CLINTSTONES – THE PREHISTORIC FIRST FAMILY

DAHLING! I WANT YOU TO DO SOMETHING SPECIAL FOR ME...

THE WHITE CAVE

JUST OPEN YOUR LI'L OL' MOUTH, AND.....

MY HUSBAND IS ENTIRELY INNOCENT....

YABBA DABBA DORK!

GLENDA SLAGG

BILL CLINTON!?! What a low-down dirty rat?!?!

A-cheatin' and a-bleatin' on Hillary, his loyal little lady!?!

With his zipper open and his flies undone — doesn't he make you wanna throw up?!?!?

I say, impeachin's too good for this two-timin' love-cheat, who's dragged the good name of the US Presidency in the world's gutter!?!?

Come on, the Ku Klux Klan!? Get your lynchin' gear on, and let's see old Bill Clinton a-danglin' from the nearest tree!!?!

I SAY hats off to naughty Bill Clinton!?!

And knickers too, if he asks me!!?

Thank Gawd there's one red-blooded male left in America, who's got the balls to go a-shaggin' and a-braggin' wherever he can!?!?!

Leave him alone, Mr Media Man!

I bet there are a million gals out there who are queuin' up to get a bit of the action in that lil' ol' Oval Office!?!

Mmmmmm!!!

ROBIN COOK!? What a low down dirty rat!!! (You've done this one. Ed.)

KATE WINSLET?!! Thank Gawd there's one gorgeous gal who's not afraid to show her curves!?!!

That's what the fellas really like — a pair of golden globes that are really Tit-anic!!? Geddit?

Everyone's going overboard for this gal!! Geddit?!

COME off it, fatty Winslet!?! No wonder the Titanic sank with you on board!?!

Hey, tell you what, Two-Ton Katie!!

Next time they film Moby Dick you can play the whale?!!!

Here's a tip from Auntie Glenda. Why don't you lay off the cream cakes, Kate, and stick to iceberg lettuce!?! Geddit?

THE QUEEN Mother, God bless you, ma'am!?!

What a wonderful example to us all!?

What courage!! What bravery!! What steadfast devotion to duty!!

It makes you proud to be British!!?!

Altogether everyone — hip, hip, hooray!! Geddit?

HAVE WE all gone stark staring bonkers!?

So, a little old lady falls over and has to go to hospital!?!

Is that a story, or what?

The only thing you can be sure about is that if it was your granny or mine, she'd be stuck on a trolley in the corridor for 48 hours before anyone noticed!?

Doesn't it make you sick?!

HERE they are, Glenda's February Full Montys.

F.W. de KLERK. South Africa's answer to Robin Cock!?!!

KEN HOM. The sexiest chef in the Orient. You can come round to my "hom" for a "wok on the wild side" anytime!?! Geddit?!

EDDIE IZZARD. Crazy name!! Crazy gal!!

Byeeeee!!

"Great idea going to Greece for our honeymoon"

The full text of President Clintstone's State of the Onion Address

The President (*takes something out of his trousers, probably an onion. Weeps copiously*): Mah fellow Americans. As the great George Washington said, when his father caught him with his chopper in his hand and a girl called Cherry: "I cannot tell a lie." Which is why I have been advised by my lawyers not to say anything further at this time. God bless Miss America! There's one hell of a dame!

(*President is ushered offstage by Mrs Hillary Roddam Clintstone*)

Mrs President Clintstone: Mah fellow Americans. In the words of the immortal Tammy Wynette, this is all a real sinister, right-wing plot to assassinate my man, and to replace him as President with some form of extra-terrestrial Newt. Don't you believe what they tell you, do you hear me? They're all liars, ah tell you.

(*Mrs Clintstone is ushered off stage by President Saddam Hussein*)

President Hussein: My fellow Iraqis (contd. p. 94)

APOLOGY

IN 1993, *Private Eye* published this front cover. We regret that due to a typographical error in the "speech bubble" the letter "f" was inadvertently printed instead of the intended letter, making the sentence both inaccurate and deeply offensive to Mr Clinton. The correct letter was, of course, an "s". We apologise for any confusion caused by our mistake.

The Daily Torygraph

Newspaper of the Year

Britain's biggest-selling quality daily · Friday February 20, 1998 · 45p

Man With Moustache and Funny Hat is Dead

A Nation Mourns Tributes Pour In

by Our Political Staff Simon Hefferlump and the late T.E. Utterlyridiculous

A MAN with a moustache and a funny voice has died aged 97.

He was widely agreed to be the finest mind of his generation and the greatest influence on British politics this century.

His decision to invade India in 1959 changed the world forever.

He later became a taxi-driver in his native Wolverhampton and enjoyed a brief period of notoriety in the late 1960s for his outspoken views on coloured immigration.

Alf Garnett was 106.

The Wisdom of Enoch

AMONG the many prophetic and extraordinary utterances of the late Oswald Powellsly were the following unforgettable contributions to Conservative political philosophy:

As Junior Health Minister 1958:

"Let's get in some coloured nurses, they're cheap."

On Britain's transport problem 1961:

"Let's get in some black bus drivers, they're cheap."

On Britain's unemployment problem 1967:

"It's time we sent these darkies home. They're costing too much."

As the Tory Party's intellectual guru, 1974:

"Vote Labour."

On the authorship of Shakespeare's plays, 1978:

"No rational person could believe that they were written by anyone other than a committee of great scholars, under the chairmanship of Queen Elizabeth the First."

On Jesus Christ, 1982:

"It is inconceivable to any sentient being that the historical figure we know as Jesus Christ was crucified. I have studied the original Greek texts, and it is clear to me that Our Lord was swallowed by a whale."

On himself, 1995:

"As I look into the future, I am filled with foreboding. I seem to see a river of garbage. I see myself foaming at the mouth, and two coloured men in white coats saying 'Come along, Mr Powell, it's time for your injection'."

Those tributes in full

Lord Grocer of Heath

"I am not going to say anything about this dreadful man. No, I'm not. So don't ask me. If you ask me, he was an appalling man. Almost as bad as Mrs Thatcher. I hope she's next."

Mr Tony Blair

"Enoch was my childhood hero, who later became a man I am proud to call both colleague and friend. He could properly be called the founder of the modern Labour Party."

The Baroness Thatch, formerly Supreme Ruler of the Universe

"Enoch was one of my greatest admirers. All his ideas about Europe and the free market came from me. He was proud to call me a friend."

The Lord Healey

"I had the greatest possible respect for myself. As an intellectual force in British politics, Enoch was second only to me."

Charles Moore

"Away from his public persona as a steely intellectual and world statesman, Enoch was in fact a warm-hearted and genial father-figure. When I was a boy at Eton, I wrote to him asking for his autograph. He responded immediately, enclosing an invoice for 100 gns. I have it framed above my desk to this day."

Letters to the Editor

What Enoch said

SIR — Your obituary of the late Enoch Powell contained a number of serious errors. As one who was actually present in person at the now famous Wolverhampton Town Hall meeting of 13 July 1968, I can vouch that the exact words used by Mr Powell on that occasion were very different indeed from the version quoted in your obituary.

Mr Powell in fact spoke throughout in his native Latin, and the key phrase which was to be so misunderstood by the media was a quotation from the great Roman author Cabbius Taxius (Chariot No. LXIVDMQ), writing in the 1st Century AD on the influx of Thracians into the city of Antioch. He said: "Timeo Danaos, et asti spumante, Tiberos fluvios rem acuit tetigisti, et ego in Arcadia vixi", which being translated means: "My fellow citizens, I tell you, all these darkies coming over here taking our jobs, they should be strung up. I had that Mark Antony in the back of the cab once." At the time, everyone in his audience understood exactly what Enoch meant, ie that he welcomed coloured immigration and the positive contribution that it could make to British life. It was only later that the great man's detractors, mostly Communists and coloured agitators, tried to make out that he was some kind of rabble-rousing racist.

A. POLOGIST
The Old Bunker
Solihull

Inside

Gay love secret of man with moustache

A SENIOR Church of England figure, Canon Eric Gropetrouser, has revealed that, while at Cambridge in the 1920s, the man with a moustache wrote a series of passionate love poems of a homo-erotic nature, using the pseudonym Enoch J. Thribb.

I saw you walking down the street
You looked so bright and gay.
But when I called round at your digs
They said you'd gone away.

(Translated from a 2nd Century fragment by the Roman tragedian Tatchellius)

© A.E. Housman

The Funeral of Mr Enoch Powell

(cont'd from p. 94)

(representing the Portaloo Apprentice Boys); Mr Simon Heffer (biographer); Mr "Mad Harry" Gobb (Millwall Supporters Association); Mr Matthew D'Ancona (Sunday Telegraph); Mr Reg Stringemup (the Wolverhampton Cab Drivers Benevolent Association); Mr Anthony Wedgwood-Benn (Parliamentary Lunatics Society); Mr Sid Himmler (Referees Association and Neasden Blackshirt Union 1937-39); Mr Charles Moore (Editor, Daily Telegraph); Mr Horace Nabarro (Editor Moustache and Moustachemen 1943-61).

TACKY

ENOCH was right. He knew this country would go to the dogs once they started allowing in foreign immigrants who would come over here with their loose morals, their all-night parties, and their drugs. I should be sent back to where I belong. It's the only language I understand.

JAPANESE AMBASSADOR LAYS WREATH

We want to build bridges

MR PUNCH BANNED
'Too shocking for kids'

by Our Media Staff **Punchtime O'Booze**

A WEST Country library has banned one of Britain's best-loved comic figures, Mr Punch, on the grounds that he is "unpleasant", "sexist" and "deeply offensive".

In a typical scene Mr Punch is groping a young assistant in his shop, while she is trying to sell sausages.

A policeman enters holding a baby, saying "Is this yours?"

Low Punch

Mr Fayed *(surely 'Punch'? Ed.)* goes berserk, grabs the policeman's truncheon and hits everyone in sight, shouting "That's the fuggin' way to do it".

However, Mr Punch had his defenders. Little Michael Cole, said, "I love him. I come in every day to watch him.

"And I think what Mr Punch is trying to say is that he loves all women and children, and wants only to be liked and given a British passport."

Michael Cole is 6.

"He adored 'Blue Peter'..."

Jap Premier's Shock Apology To All Sun Readers

Original Japanese text – read sideways

Dear Sun Readers:

On behalf of the people of Japan, I would like to say that I am very sorry for everything that happened in the Second World War, particularly for Hiroshima, Nagasaki and the Bridge Over The River Kwai.

But hopefully all that is now in the past and the Japanese people can now show their deep contrition by buying up your famous Millennium Dome.

Yours sincerely,

MR TAMAGOTCHI, Prime Minister of Japan
(as dictated by Alistair Campbell)

ON OTHER PAGES

NOT ON OTHER PAGES

● **Murdoch Apologises to Britain for Sun**

The Daily Hellograph

Newspaper of the Year

Britain's biggest-selling quality   Friday, March 6, 1998   **45p**

Rich Fat Woman 'Not Very Ill'

Nation In State Of Shock

by Our Man in Mustique Roundtheclock O'Booze

A RICH fat woman on holiday in the luxury Caribbean palm-fringed paradise hideaway island of Mustique yesterday felt "slightly ill" after an agreeable dinner.

The rich fat woman was immediately flown to the nearby luxury, palm-fringed hideaway hospital of Barbados, where her condition was later said to be "fat, rich and not very ill".

Our medical correspondent Dr Stutterfraud writes: We doctors have long known that a woman of 67 is prone to regular attacks of not feeling as well as you might. If she is wealthy or overweight, the condition may be exacerbated.

Smoking and drinking are likely to make the condition fatal, although in this case there is nothing to suggest that the patient has any cause for alarm.

Other factors such as unrequited love for Captain Townsend, a failed marriage to Lord Snowdon or an unfortunate affair with a much younger man, like Roddy Llewellyn will all help to prolong the article, and can often be very useful as a means of boosting circulation.

Inside

A Doctor writes

Dempster's Syndrome

AS A DOCTOR I am not often asked about this very rare condition, which is thought to affect only one person in the entire world. What happens is that the patient is stopped by the police while driving his car in what appears to be an inebriated fashion. When asked to give a blood sample, he refuses, saying: "How dare you! Do you realise who I am? I am married to Lady Camilla Pratt-Dumpster, the daughter of the Duke of Leedsh."

When asked again, the patient suddenly remembers that he has a lifelong allergy to needles (or *Hypodermis dumpsteris implausibilis*, as it is now known to the medical profession).

At this point the officer may well say: "I don't like pricks much either."

However, if you are worried about drink driving, you should try claiming to have Dempster's Syndrome — though it must be stressed that this remedy will not prove effective in all courts.

© A. Doctor 1998

HUGE ASTEROID HITS HEADLINE

by Our Space Staff Phil Space

AN enormous asteroid last night hurtled on to the front page of the world's newspapers creating a tidal wave of relief amongst global newsmen.

"We were getting very frightened that our world would end since we didn't have any stories," said stargazer Charles "Patrick" Moore. "But then I was just watching the Sky TV at Night when I noticed this huge asteroid story coming towards me."

"It was so big even I could not miss it. First there was just space and then suddenly an enormous lump of matter crashed into the front page measuring 10 inches across 4 columns."

Scientists predicted that the asteroid story will have incredible side effects including:

● **The blocking out of all other important stories, eg Kate Winslet's new boyfriend.**

● **Vast quantities of graphics flooding the world's papers.**

● **The Sun exploding.**

● **Alan Coren taking a sideways look at what might happen when the asteroid hits Cricklewood.**

"The bacon's off"

AUTUMN BOOKS

Sir Charles Moore
by Peter Ackroyd

A stunning new biography of the late 20th Century saint who played a leading role in both politics and the church, until he fell out with his patron King Conrad the Black who ordered his execution in the notorious Tower at Canary Wharf.

The Female Enoch
by Dr Germaine Drear

In a polemical tirade, Dr Drear savages modern women for being obsessed by sex. She attacks them for ignoring their roles as mothers and homemakers, and lays the blame squarely at the door of sex-obsessed '60s feminists like Germaine Greer.

EXCLUSIVE!

HALLO! is proud to present these heartwarming pictures of the Duchess of York's recent skiing holiday. They show a different side of the Duchess and offer a unique and charming perspective on this ever popular member of the Royal Family. ■

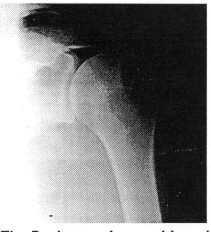

The Duchess enjoys a chipped bone in her right shoulder

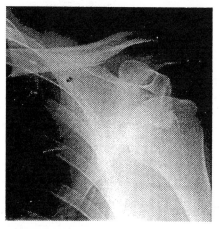

The Duchess relaxes in the Radiography Department

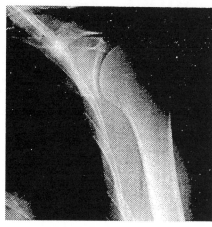

The Duchess takes us inside her delightful upper torso

'REPLACE TESTS WITH CONTINUAL ASSESSMENT'

New demand by English Head

by Our Education Staff **R.R. Arr**

A FORMAL demand for an end to "unfair tests" has been lodged by the England cricket captain, Mr Michael Atherton B.A. Cantbat *(shurely 'Cantab'? Ed)*.

"These tests are completely unrepresentative of English players' cricket ability. We should be assessed throughout the year on our performance in the nets and not judged on a very stressful one-off five-day trial."

He continued: "Players of enormous ability are failing through no fault of their own. A test is an artificial situation where an individual is suddenly expected to bat or bowl well on the spur of the moment."

He concluded: "If we had had continual assessment monitoring our performance in practice matches we would have won the Ashes and would be three-nil up in the current series against the West Indies."

LATE SCORE

England (Batting Module 1)	3,492 for 0 wickets
Stewart	2,342 units completed
Atherton	1,150 units completed

Result: England Pass

Lord Lairgover's Press Guide

❶ No article shall be permitted to appear which may be deemed in any way to invade the privacy of Her Majesty's Government.

❷ No article shall be permitted to appear concerning the sexual mores of any serving minister of the Crown since these are not in the public interest.

❸ No article shall be permitted to appear referring to the relationship between Mr Robin Cock and Mrs Goneril Regan, since their private lives are not a matter of public interest.

❹ Should any journalist ever again dare to refer to the fact that I ran off with Donald Dewar's wife in 1976, that same person shall be taken from this place, whereinsoever that may be, and hanged by the neck until he or she is dead.

❺ Have you got that, you bastards?

Given this day under the Great Seal of Lord Lairgover of Glenmorangie
Cardinal Woosey
Hampton Court

Whilst doing a long-overdue clearout at the offices of Ireland's oldest and most respected school of dance, Mrs O' Hara made a terrible discovery...

"Jane, darling, I'm just on my way home. I shouldn't be too late..."

E.P. MCHENRY

Introducing the Eye's New Star Columnist

SALLY JOCKSTRAP

The Voice of Sport

I WATCHED the British cricket team on the television last night. Honestly! who selected this shower and left out Ian Wright and Alan Shearer? He needs his head examined. Britain were lucky to get away with a 0-0 draw.

I'VE BEEN a Sheffield Tuesday fan all my life — but even I have to admit they are never going to win the way they are playing at the moment. When I went down to watch them at Twickenham, Steve Davis was distinctly off form with breaks of 12, 22 and 31.

WHAT'S gone wrong with Tim Henman? No wonder the boss of Arsenal Hotspur is keeping him on the bench *(cont. p. 94)*

(cont. p. 94)

Those Winter Olympics Results In Full ⬤⬤⬤

Men's Snowballing
Gold: Spliff Rizla *(Canada)*
Silver: Mario Juana *(Mexico)*
Bronze: Hashish Baksheesh *(Pakistan)*

Mr Rizla was later disqualified when traces of snow were discovered up his nose.

Women's 2000m Downhill Ice Sumo
Gold: Poppy Grower (Australia)
Silver: Ko-Ko Kain (South Korea)
Bronze: Ellesse Dee (France)

The remainder of the day's programme was abandoned due to the wrong kind of snow on the mountain. The BBC will therefore be continuing with full coverage of the day's snow presented by Desmond Main-Lynam.

JOBS VACANT
Scum de la Scum

GEC-MARCONI are looking for a senior management executive to co-ordinate and oversee their sales initiative in the Middle East.

The successful candidate should have suitable experience as a shady spiv with a wide knowledge of lying, cheating and sucking up to the towelheads.

An added attraction to the employer would be some experience in running a seedy health hydro and procuring high-class tarts for wealthy clients.

Only Jonathan Aitken need apply.

© *Crime de la Crime*

"Take a Valentine card to yourself..."

ROBIN COOK

Ken Pyne

47

Lines Written On The Non-Awarding Of A Knighthood To Scotland's Premier Actor, 🏵 Mr Sean Connery 🏵

by William McGonagall

'TWAS in the year nineteen hundred and ninety eight
That the British nation failed to appreciate
The genius of Scotland's greatest actor
Whose support for the SNP was to prove the decisive
       factor.

But hold, I am telling my tale too fast.
It behoves us now to go back into the past.
Young Sean Connery began his story
Delivering milk to the folk of Edinburgh both Labour
       and Tory.

(In those days the young milkman had no political
       affiliation
He was happy just to deliver silvertop and cans
       of Carnation.)

But then he was spotted by the great director
       Cubby Broccoli
Who said "I will make you a star earning lots of lolly.
You will play the part of 007, James Bond."
"Isn't he an upper-class Englishman?" young Sean
       did respond.

"Never ye mind," said the mogul, "This spy
From now on will be saying 'Och aye'!"
"Ok," said Sean, "I will give it a go."
Which is how he made his debut in *Dr No*.

Many were the films which were soon to ensue –
From Russia With Love, Thunderball and *Goldfinger* too.
The series became even more popular than *Lassie*
Each one prefaced with a song by Miss Shirley Bassey.

This incredible success gave Sean a luxurious life-style
And so the patriotic young Scot decided to become a
       tax exile.
Sean Connery then became the toast of Hollywood
Playing in a number of films which were not very good.

Eventually lots of people suggested that Sean become
       a knight.
"Arise Sir 007." Yes, that sounded right!
Those who opposed the plan were somewhat fewer.
But they were led by the influential Donald Dewar.

Said he, "Why should we do this man a favour?
He told folk to vote SNP, not Labour."
Of course, canny Donald did not admit this to press.
Rather, he told them it was because Sean likes to beat
       up anything in a dress.

This was why Scotland's finest son was struck off the
       list, er...
And thus he was doomed to remain just plain
       Connery, Mr.

© The Estate of the Late William Rees-McGonagall

COUNTRYSIDE UNITES

We demand the right to moan

MCC TO REMAIN 'BORES ONLY'
Shock vote outrages country

by **Lunchtime Score O'Booze**

THE WORLD's oldest bores' club, the MCC, is to keep its doors firmly shut to anyone who is not a bore.

This was the shock result of a poll of the club's 18,000 members, who last night voted unanimously to retain the MCC's coveted all-bore status.

Said the leader of the pro-bore faction, 107-year-old Mr L.B.W. Crasher-Grimblett: "I have nothing personally against people who are not bores — indeed, I am married to one. However, there must be a place where a chap can go, secure in the knowledge that he will be surrounded only by bores like himself."

Sir Timothy Rice is 98 not out.

What You Get For Your £70,000 A Year

● Red and yellow tie
● Red face
● Er... that's it.

Deirdre Spart, Co-Chair of the Hackney Downs Women-Only Cricket Club, comments:

Once again in a totally sickening and predictable act of sport-fascism, the paternalist cricket establishment has instituted their own gender apartheid on the game's oppressed minority, i.e. women. Tony Banks is totally right when he threatens to abolish the MCC and to build much-needed, affordable housing for single parents and same-sex couples on the hated greenfield site that is currently occupied by the Male Chauvinist Conspiracy (i.e. MCC) which is totally *(cont. p. 94)*

"So we thought we'd make you feel at home..."

Test Match Special

Christopher Martin Jenkins *(for it is he)*: And we welcome listeners with the astonishing news that Geoffrey Boycott is out. Geoffrey?

Borecott: 'Appen I've never been out like this. It's a reet disgrace. These BBC t'boogers tuppeny ha'porth bread wi' nowt taken out, t'BBC know booger all about t'battering. Y'can't treat t'woman with kid gloves. You've got to get stook in and show her who's t'boss. Once you've got your eye in you can knock her's out and hit t'lass all round t'bedroom. Aye, they don't make t'wife-beaters like they used to. I can remember at Headingley in 1963 *(Cont 94KHz)*

Moo Labour!

I've always been a lover of the countryside

It's a moo-turn!

New-Look Radio Bore

An at-a-glance guide to the radio station that's really going places (downmarket).

COURT CIRCULAR

SANDRINGHAM

His Royal Highness the Prince of Wales last night received Lady Camilla Parker-Bowles into his private apartments. She was accompanied by two overnight bags and a number of toilet requisites. There was a formal legover followed by the ceremonial smoking of a cigarette.

The Prince was attended by Sir Alan Fitztightly, the Master of the Royal Revels and Keeper of the Something For The Weekend.

A DRAMATIC shake-up in Radio 4 schedules, the biggest since last week, has provoked a storm of protest amongst hard-core Radio Four listeners (Sir Herbert and Lady Laetitia Gusset, Co-Chair of The Dorset Countryside Alliance Committee).

Long-running programmes to face the axe include:

● "Does He Eat Toast?"
● "The Toast Programme"
● "Medium Toast"

● "Your Toast Tonight"
● "The Toast Quiz"

Controversial new programmes include:

● The Toast File
● Down Your Toast
● Sport on Toast (with Martin Bashir)
● Afternoon Tcast
● Desert Island Toast.

(That's enough of this feature. Ed.)

The Times Guide To Sleep (adapted from the best-selling book "Z-z-z-z" by Dr Stothardford)

Pt. 94: How to get a good night's sleep

1. Purchase copy of Times (20p on Monday).
2. Open at any page.
3. Start reading.
4. Hey presto — you're asleep!
5. Z-z-z-z...

© *The China Daily*

Queen's Proposals For New-Look Royals

BY OUR COURT STAFF KENNETH ROSEWITHOUTTRACE

THE most radical shake-up of the monarchy in 2000 years has been proposed by the Royal Family in response to the death of Diana, Princess of Wales™.

Following last year's barrage of criticism that the Royal Family was "out of touch", "anachronistic" and "stuck in a medieval time warp", the Queen has personally initiated a series of "drastic" and "radical" moves to bring the monarchy "into the 21st Century".

Those Shock Changes In Full

1. The Union Flag will fly above Buckingham Palace on alternate Wednesdays to give tourists something to photograph.

2. Those meeting the Queen below the rank of Marquess will no longer be required to walk backwards for more than 15 paces.

3. A major shake-up in the official Order of Precedence will result in the younger daughters of an Earl no longer taking automatic precedence over bishops who do not serve in the House of Lords.

4. The honorific title of Princess will be withdrawn from Fergie's ghastly children, whatever their names are.

5. Er…

6. …that's it.

Blair's Proposals For New-Look Royals

BY OUR POLITICAL STAFF ALISTAIR CAMPBELL

MR TONY Blair has personally authorised a number of minor reforms intended to "modernise" the image of the Royal Family, to bring it more into line with the needs of a vibrant, pivotal country recovering from the trauma of the death of Diana, Princess of Wales™.

The "Blair Reforms" have been drawn up following consultation with focus groups in all parts of the country (Islington).

Those Minor Changes In Full

1. Royal Family to travel by bicycle only, except for State Opening of Parliament when Queen may be permitted to use public transport.

2. Prime Minister and wife to take precedence over Royalty at all official functions.

3. The weekly "audience" with the Prime Minister to be held in future at 10, Downing Street (Queen to attend on foot).

4. Royal Corgis to be fed on Kwik Save Doggo-chunks (27p) to bring them into line with Dutch Royal dogs.

5. Royal art collection to be rehoused in the apartments of Lord Lairg, to bring it into line with all other public collections.

6. Buckingham Palace to be bulldozed to bring it into line with the ground.

7. Royal Family to be shot in Bolshevik-style atrocity in Forest of Windsor.

Let's Parler Franglais

No. 94: The Official Inquiry Into The Death of Diana, Princess of Wales.

Juge Coqauvin (*pour c'est lui*): Ah, Monsieur Fayed, qu'est-ce-que-c'est, cette garbage about une conspiracie, avec regard to le white Fiat, Mossad et MI5?

Fayed: Fug-moi! C'est vrai, what I said, vous fuggin' idiot Français.

Juge: Où est le proof de votre pack of lies, s'il vous plaît?

Fayed: Je suis le fuggin' boss de Harrods, le plus fameux department-store du monde, où on peut snap up beaucoup de bargains. Pour example, dans le Departement de Piano, au second floor, nous avons un Steinway Taiwanese pour seulement £5,000. Et aussi, un emerald tiara magnifique, le property de Monsieur Tiny Rowland …

Juge: Tais-toi, buffoon Egyptien. Où est le proof?

Fayed: Vous voulez fuggin' proof? Je vous donnerai fuggin' proof. C'est tous dans le nouvel edition du Punch, seulement £1.

Juge: Monsieur le gendarme, arrestez cet homme. Il n'a pas de passport Anglais.

(*Les flics drag the accused Mr Fayed au cells*)

Fayed: Attendez un fuggin' moment, vous fuggin' judge. J'ai ici un envelope brun, avec votre nom on it.

© 100-Miles-an-Hour Kington

LEGAL QUERIES

The New Compensation Scheme

From Mrs Ethel Prunehat:

Since seeing Lord Irvine of Lairgover on the television, I have been diagnosed as suffering from traumatic stress. Who do I write to, to claim my £5 million in compensation?

Old Bore writes: Thanks to the Law Commission's new scheme, you can pick up a claim form from your local Benefits Office and return it with a doctor's certificate to the Lord Chancellor's Department. Compensation will be given to you immediately.

From Mr Nigel Prunehat:

When my mother was traumatised by seeing Lord Lairgover on the television, I was unfortunately out of the room making tea. I immediately became traumatised at the thought of not being able to claim compensation for being traumatised. Can I claim compensation for not being allowed to claim compensation?

Old Bore writes: Indeedy-doody. Just follow the procedure explained above, and hey presto, you're almost as rich as Lord Lairg himself!

From Mr Reginald Prunehat:

My wife and son have suddenly become millionaires, meanwhile I am landed with a huge tax bill. Can I claim compensation for the trauma of having to pay for everyone else's compensation?

"I'd be 63 today, had I lived"

IS BLAIR PLANNING SECRET CONVERSION TO TORYISM?

by Our Religious
Affiliairs Correspondent
Father Ted Heath

THE WORLD will be shocked to learn that the Prime Minister Mr Tony Blair has recently been making secret visits to Conservative Central Office to find out what to do next.

Only last week he was spotted purchasing a number of tracts, including "The Way Forward For The Welfare State" by Father Peter Lilley, "How To Privatise The Armed Forces" by Monsignor Redwood, and "Let's Hang All The Scroungers" by Dom Miguel di Portillo S.J.

Ad Major Dei Gloriam

Blair has also been seen worshipping at the shrine of Our Lady of Thatcher in Chester Square, where he was observed kneeling at the feet of the Blessed Virago Margaret.

This blatant act of Maggiolatry has so shocked extreme members of Blair's congregation that some of them have denounced him as "a crypto-Right Footer who will lead this country into the arms of the Treaty of Rome".

But last night a Downing Street spokesman denied that the Prime Minister was about to become a Conservative. "He already is one," he said.

POINTS OF VIEW

Silly Presenter: Hullo. We've had a lot of letters this week about the repeat of *Look In My Drawers*, the 1970s' sitcom about a furniture factory in Nottingham.

Silly Reader: Dear Points of View.It was wonderful to see my favourite sitcom back on the BBC. Well done the BBC for showing it again!Could we see, just once more, please Ann, the hilarious scene where Mr Wilmot glues his trousers to the fork-lift truck? *Mrs Yentob of Shepherds Bush.*

Presenter: My pleasure, Mrs Yentob.

(Clip shows man gluing trousers to forklift truck)

Presenter: Last week saw the launch of the new 39-part "fly on the wall" documentary *Happy Eaters?*, following the lives of three school-leavers as they start their first job in a motorway service cafe. Typical of thousands of letters, all in praise of the programme, was one from Mrs Wyatt of Wood Lane, London.

Reader: Congratulations to the BBC for *Happy Eaters?*, another superb programme from good old Auntie! I shall not be going out on Thursdays ever again, so long as this brilliant series lasts. Can we please see again the unforgettable sequence where Jacqui gives the wrong change to a customer.

Presenter: You certainly can, Mrs Wyatt!

(Clip of girl giving wrong change to customer)

Presenter: Finally, a note of criticism, from a viewer who found something she didn't like!

Reader: Come off it BBC! Why can't you ever surprise us by producing a bad programme and giving us something to complain about? The BBC is fantastic, and so is its wonderful Director-General John Birt. Could you please make my day by showing a picture of him? *Mrs J. Birt, Portland Place.*

Presenter: Anything to oblige, Mrs B! And for what it's worth, I agree with everything you say!

(Still photo of His Holiness the Birt of Birts appears, accompanied by solemn music)

Presenter: If you have any comments on any BBC programmes, make sure they are positive, or they won't get read out!

ST CAKES 'NOT ELITIST' SAY INSPECTORS

by Our Education Staff
Mr Micro Chips

TOP Midlands public school St Cakes (motto "Quis donat entrat" -"Who pays gets in") has been praised by an official report for its "non-elitist character".

The £28,000-a-term boarding school is described by inspectors as "open, friendly, relaxed and classless".

Said headmaster Mr Kipling: "I am delighted by the report. St Cakes has always been open to anyone. We are not snobbish in the slightest. On the contrary, our principles are entirely egalitarian. We allow entry to anyone irrespective of colour, class or creed — but we do draw the line at poverty."

Mr Kipling makes exceedingly large amounts of money.

Leave My Bosses Alone

I HOLD no brief for Mr Rupert Murdoch. As far as I am concerned, he is just the man who pays my wages.

But when I see the media all going for him, just because he doesn't want to publish Chris Patten's silly, boring memoirs, it makes me want to stand up and shout "Hang on, what has Mr Murdoch ever done to you?"

As far as I am concerned, it is entirely his own business which writers he chooses to sack, and which he chooses to allow to continue writing their column in the Times.

Similarly, I hold no brief for the BBC and Mr James Boyle, head of Radio Four. As far as I am concerned, they are just the people who sign my salary cheque for doing the brilliant Mid-Week programme (now, as part of the great Radio Four facelift, re-named "Midweek" and starting at the slightly later time of 9.07).

writes Glibby Purves

But when I see the media all ganging up to have a go at the new Radio Four, just because it's the same as the old one except slightly more boring, it makes me want to stand up and shout: "Hang on, what has Jimmy Boyle ever done to you? Don't you realise that the BBC is one of the greatest institutions in the entire history of civilisation? And it has a perfect right to choose which presenters should be sacked, and which should be allowed to continue presenting their superb, though slightly shorter Mid-Week programmes just after the nine o'clock news."

And now, to cap it all, Mr Rupert Murdoch has made a brilliant and courageous speech attacking the brilliant and courageous BBC. Oh dear. What on earth am I to say? I think I had better keep quiet on this one and write about my life in the Suffolk countryside.

© *Glibtrash Productions, The Times*

Why I Love China

by William Rees-Mogg

ALL MY life I have loved China. Even when I was at Charterhouse China was my grand passion. I have studied it and made it a field of particular expertise. So when the proprietor rang me to say "William, I want you to write a piece in praise of China," I was only too happy to oblige.

The first piece I ever bought, at a Church fete in Hinton Blewitt in 1923, was a willow-pattern Wedgwood teapot. The lid was missing and there was a small chip in the spout. But apart from that it was exquisite.

(Is this what you wanted,

Rupert? It seems a bit odd. I could do another piece on Staffordshire next week, if you like. Gillian has a lovely pair of spaniels on her escritoire.)

The New Times Crossword In Full

ACROSS
1. The greatest country in the world (5)

DOWN
1. Wonderful people (7)

SOLUTION

NEW LOOK QUEEN

Oi! Phil! You wanna Guinness or what?

THOSE MEMBERS OF PANEL 2000 IN FULL

Blair appoints Committee of Cool

THE following have been appointed by the Prime Minister Mr Tony Blair to sit on the prestigious Government Advisory Committee for the Re-brandification of the United Kingdom (Now Cool Britannia Plc).

Mr Derek Fatchett MP (chairman and non-entity)

Mr Tinky Winky (BBC co-ordinator)

Ms Mel C (international recording artiste)

Ms Stella Topes (daughter of Sir Spigismond and world leading fashion designer)

Ms Mariella Frostrup (broadcaster, star of Channel 5's "No one's Watching" show)

TV's **Inspector Morse** (senior police officer and Mozart specialist)

Sir Christopher Evans OBE (friend of Gazza)

Kennedy (formerly Nigella Kennedy-Lawson of the Times)

Diana's Butler (fill in name)

The cast of the Full Monty *(That's enough "cool" people. Ed.)*

"And anyway you're only allowed to dress casually on Fridays"

"Mum, Dad, I've got something to tell you — I'm a homophobe"

Blair's 4-Point Plan to end the Welfare State

by Our New Labour Staff **Dame Edna Beveridge**

MR TONY Blair today unveiled Harriet Harman's radical scheme to implement Frank Field's plans to abolish the welfare state, thus saving Britain £2000 billion a year.

How it will work:

1. Everyone will get a job.
2. This will mean that they don't need welfare any more.
3. Er...
4. That's it.

MUDDLED ENGLAND GOES ON THE MARCH

by Our Cannabis Correspondents
Gunter Grass and **Norman Stoned**

THEY CAME in their thousands, young and old, rich and poor, long haired and slightly less long haired, with just one message for London: "Er..."

D'ye Ken John Peel On Radio One

Said the leader of the march's organisers, Dame Rosie Buypot. "We've all had a spliffing afternoon and we've really shown people that smoking dope is a traditional part of the British way of life. What finer sight could there be than a group of bearded men in pink trousers sitting down together and lighting up a joint."

Tally High!

Continued Dame Rosie, "You cannot criminalise a whole section of society just because they want to go hunting for dope in the middle of the afternoon.

"People like us do not normally go on demonstrations. We prefer to stay in bed reading the Independent and trying to make sense of section two."

Dame Rosie Buypot is 78.

ALL COUNTRIES MEET THE EURO CONVERGENCE CRITERIA — IT'S OFFICIAL!

by Our EU Staff **Benny Lux**

CHAMPAGNE corks were popping in Brussels last night when it was announced that all 15 countries in the EU had met the very strict conditions laid down for joining the Euro.

Sir Leon Anti-Britten, Vice-President of the European Commission, said: "This gives the lie to all those doubters and Europhobes who claimed that countries like Greece, Italy, Portugal, Spain, Austria, Luxembourg, Holland, Bel-gium, Ireland, Sweden, Denmark, Finland, France and Germany had no chance of qualifying."

Those Really Tough Criteria In Full

1. To qualify for entry, all countries must fill in the appropriate form EC/1998/462, and send it to Mr J. Santer.

2. All countries must answer the questions on the form to the satisfaction of Mr J. Santer. The questions are:

   a) What is the name of your country?

   b) Would you like to join the Euro?

3. Er...

4. That's it.

CLINTON IN AFRICA

Day 8: President to arrive in Uganda for discussions.

18:00 Visits capital of Legova to meet President Bonko Bonko.

19:00 Visits settlement of Rumpi Pumpi.

20:00 Meets members of Totti Dance Troupe.

21:00 Formal reception with Chief Gobblo of the Wanafaki Tribe.

22:00 President flies undone *(surely 'home'? Ed.)*

Coming soon: Disney's Frankenstein

WORLD'S GREATEST TRAGEDY

—●—

NO BRITISH SURVIVORS IN TITANIC DISASTER

—●—

by Our Man in Hollywood Lunchtime O'Verboard

BRITAIN was in a state of shock last night as news came through that a group of upper-class Englishwomen had all sunk without trace on their journey to America.

Never had a group of actresses in period costume set out from these shores with such high hopes.

Bands had played, Union flags had waved and the *Daily Telegraph* had run enormous articles for days beforehand headed "Confident Predictions of British Successes in Motion Picture Awards", "Watch Out America, The Super-Brits Are Coming" and "Blimey — It's Kate Winsalot!" (pics pages 1, 3, 5, 94).

WOMEN AND CHILDREN LAST

The whole nation followed the progress of the British hopefuls as they headed across the ocean towards the New World.

But then, early in the morning on 23 March, disaster struck.

Out of the darkness loomed the largest and most expensive film ever made.

This was the film which they all said was unsinkable.

But they were wrong. The vast bulk of the Titanic smashed into the British hopefuls, who all disappeared below the waves of the crowd without a murmur.

These poor British women and children will never be heard of again, and experts predict that they will be washed up in a matter of days.

Those who perished included victims from all classes:

FIRST CLASS

Dame Judith Dench O.B.E. Dame Judi liked to dress up in the Crown Jewels and pretend to be Queen Victoria.

Lady Violet Bonham Carter. Lady Helena was connected to the grandest of British families and liked to take off all her clothes.

Lady Kate Winslet, 11. Sweet, innocent child who also liked to take off all her clothes.

STEERAGE

A group of five working-class men, all called **Monty**, who particularly liked to take off all their clothes.

The only British survivor of the disaster was **Miss Anne Dudley**, a little-known musician.

"I could not believe my luck," she said. "When the Titanic struck, I thought it was all over for me.

"But then, miraculously, someone threw me an Oscar to cling to and I somehow managed to scramble out of the wreckage and into the headlines."

LOST   **LOST**   **LOST**

Dame Judith Dench   Lady Violet Bonham Carter   Lady Kate Winslet

HOW THEY ARE RELATED

da Vinci

di Caprio

Direct Descent

Leonardo da Vinci
|
Sir Leon da Brittani
|
Sir Leonardo di Lotteri
|
Sir Lenny da Henry
|
Lady Lena Zavaroni
|
Signor Kipliana (" 'e make exceedingly good Torti")
|
Francis Ford Capri
|
Leonardo di Crapio
(shurely "Caprio"? Ed)

Tchavdar

Ready, Steady, Cook-Up!
with TV's Robin Cook

Today's Recipe: Palestinian Artichokes

Ingredients: One bucket salt; one old wound.

Directions: Stir everything up and bring blood to the boil.

Tomorrow: Peace Pudding (off)

![SOCCER] **THOSE KNEEGATE TAPES**

pp 1, 2, 3, 4, 5, 7-26 (Bonus page no. 94)

■**FOLLOWING the sensational revelations in last week's Eye, we are proud to bring you another instalment of the filthy tapes which illustrate the moral depravity of the men they call "the Sleazebags of Soccer" (Neasden Manager Ron Knee, 59, and his Chairman, Brig. Buffy Cohen).**

Posing as a bona-fide Croatian lap-dancer, top *News-of-the-Eye* investigative reporter **E.I. Erewego** trapped the disgusting duo into shock revelations that have rocked Neasden football club to its foundations and forced their shock resignation.

"You're gonna get your head smashed in"

Dressed only in fishnet tights and a gold-lamé tape recorder, our award-winning reporter approached the pornographic pair in the Wayfarer's Lounge Suite of the Novotel in Hammersmith. The following exchanges then took place:

Erewego: Hullo big boys, would you like me to dance on your laps? By the way, I'm a big soccer fan, me. What do you think of Neasden Football Club?

Knee: They are all useless bastards. Except Wally Foot, who is a Goody-Two-Shoes, or rather Goody-One-Shoe, since he only has one leg, ha ha ha!

Cohen: Nice one, Ron, let's have another drink. Over here, Sambo! Three large Armagnacs and put it on the club slate.

Erewego: What do you think of your fans, dearie?

Knee: Well, I wouldn't want to shag that Doris Bonkers. Like all Neasden birds, she's a real dog.

Cohen: And Sid, he's a total moron. What a thick git! He must need his head examined to pay £50 for a season to watch the Squirrels being kicked around the park every Saturday afternoon.

Erewego: Could you speak up a bit, and talk into my right breast?

Knee: Pleasure's mine, darling.

(Tape is muffled for a while)

Erewego: And what about the strip?

Cohen: Yeah, get on with it, get your kit off.

Erewego: No, I mean the away-shirts you keep changing.

Cohen: Yeah, it's a great scam. We ship 'em in from Taiwan. They're made by blind kiddies, 6 years old, we pay 'em 2p a year for 1000 shirts, and we flog 'em for £60 each to lads like young Kevin Bonkers. Can't be bad! I thought you were going to get your kit off, sweetheart.

Erewego: Oh, look at the time. I must be off. I've got... er... a plane to catch, I mean train, er...

(Sound of Knee falling over and throwing up, as hotel pianist Vladimir Rubinstein [Sidney Potts] strikes up with Strangers In The Night [arranged Potts])

The News Of The Screws says

What could be more disgusting than ourselves? *(Surely these two evil men who have dragged the good name of soccer into the gutter'?)*

POETRY CORNER

Lines on the Death of Sir Ronald Miller, chief jokewriter to Mrs Thatcher

So. Farewell then
Sir Ronald Miller.

U turn if you like.
But the lady's not for
Turning.

That was your joke.

Now that Mr Blair
Has come to power
U must be
Turning
In your grave.

E.J. Thribb (17½)

NEW OLD SAYINGS

One U-turn deserves another

In Memoriam: Lines on the appointment of Mr Wilby as Editor of the *New Statesman*

So. Peter Wilby.

You are
Editor of
The *New Statesman*.

Or at least
You soon
Wilby.

And then you
Won't be.

E.J. Thribb (circulation 17½)

NEW OLD SAYINGS

You can't hurry luvvies

In Memoriam Kenneth Wood, inventor of the "Kenwood" Mixer and the Reversible Toaster.

So. Farewell then
Ken Wood.

Inventor of the
Reversible
Toaster.

Reversible the of
Inventor
Wood Ken.

Then farewell
So.

E.J. Thribb, inventor of the
Reversible Poem (½71)

In Memoriam Frank Muir, TV Panellist, Writer of *Take It From Here* and author of *The Frank Muir Book*

So. Farewell then
Frank Muir

With your white hair,
Pink bow tie and
Funny
Way of talking.

"Every one's a
Fruit and nut case."

That was your
Catchprase.

But now you have been
Taken From Here.

E.J. Thribb (17¾)

NEW OLD SAYINGS

To err is Harman

NEW OLD SAYINGS

Strike while the weather is hot

In Memoriam: Lines on the decision to terminate Renault's popular Nicole and Papa advertising campaign

So. Farewell
Then.
Nicole and
Papa.

"Papa!" That was
Nicole's catchphrase.

"Nicole!" That was
Papa's.

Keith's mum
Hopes you have
Now made
Enough money

To buy a
Decent car.

E.J. Thribbio (17½ mpg)

NEW OLD SAYINGS

Marry in haste, repent in leisurewear

Lines on the retirement of Sir Peter O'Sullevan, BBC racing commentator

So. Farewell then
Peter O'Sullevan.
The BBC's
Voice of
Racing.

"They're off!"
That was
Your catchphrase
And now

You are too.

E.J. Thribb, the "Voice of
Poetry" (aged 17-1)

NEW OLD SAYINGS

Time waits for no Mandelson

NEW OLD SAYINGS

Better Lite Than Never

Lines On The Retirement Of Mr Michael Atherton From The Captaincy of the England Cricket Team (1993-8)

So. Farewell then
Michael Atherton
English cricket captain.
3, 0, 1, 13*, 0.

Those were your scores.

"Oh no, it's slipped
Through Athers's fingers
Again."

That was your
Dropped catch phrase.

E.J. Thribb (17½ not out,
after 3 hours)

Lines Written On The Announcement That Mr Nigel Kennedy Wishes In Future To Be Known Simply As "Kennedy".

So. Farewell then
Nigel Kennedy
Famous Violinist.

From now on the world
Will know you
Only as
"Kennedy".

Keith said that
In years to come
Everyone will remember
Where they were
When they heard
The news about
"Kennedy".

"Thribb"
(formerly E.J. Thribb, 17½)

NEW OLD SAYINGS

Where there's Mac there's brass

In Memoriam: Tammy Wynette, the Queen of Country and Western

So. Farewell then
Tammy Wynette.

Famous country
And western
Singer.

"Stand by your man" –
That was your
Catchphrase.

And, with all five of
Your husbands,

You did.

E.J.T.H.R.I.B.B. (17½)

NEW OLD SAYINGS

Two Heads are better than one

THE PEOPLE'S PRINCE

by Dame Sylvie Krin

From the best-selling pen that brought you *Born To Be Queen*, *Heir of Sorrows* and *La Dame Aux Camillas*.

THE STORY SO FAR:

Charles and Camilla are hosting a prestigious "Weekend of Culture and Reflection" at Sandringham.

Now read on...

"THE organic pheasant was delicious, your Majesty." Sir Nicholas Arsota laid down his pearl-handled knife and fork, dabbing his lips with his monogrammed damask napkin.

"I'm so very glad you like it. I shot it myself with my organic gun."

The Prince surveyed his dining table, replete with shining silver, the finest Waldegrave dinner service (given to his great-grandmother by the Archduke Hussey of Pilsen-Holstein), and gleaming goblets filled to the brim with Chateau Poundsbury 1997, Charles's own award-winning Dorset vineyard.

Sandringham had played the host to many a gracious gathering in olden days gone by, thought Charles, but never had it witnessed a scene as glittering as this.

Here, he mused, was the veritable cream of all the finest talents of his realm.

There to his right was the silver-haired Viscount Ipswich, diplomat-turned-art historian, holding forth to the beautiful Lady Carla Interpolizzi, the heiress to the Asda fortune.

"My dear, have you heard the new Oasis album? It's really awfully good..."

And there to Charles's left was the urbane, suave financier Lord Grapes of Rothschild, who had recently intervened to save a priceless Legova sculpture, the Page Three Graces, for the national collection of which he was Chairman.

He was talking earnestly about the problems of the strong pound to the sleeping figure of Camilla Parker-Bowles.

"Hang on," thought Charles, "this isn't right. Surely Camilla should be listening intently to the words of wisdom from the great economic genius."

He gave her a discreet kick on the shins under the table, whereupon she woke up with a start and reached instinctively for her packet of Princess Margaret Full Strength.

"God, this wine's filthy, Charles," she said, lost in a cloud of smoke. "What is it?"

"WHAT is it?" asked Lady Harrods, the venerable, 96 year old architectural historian, as the young musicians of the Tamagotchi String Quartet struck up with an arrangement of the theme tune to The Full Monty.

"It's Vivaldi, I think," Charles replied, "they're awfully good, aren't they?"

At this moment there was a flurry at the doorway, and the butler entered to announce the belated arrival of the chief guest of the weekend.

Everyone craned forward in anticipation. This was the moment they had all been waiting for. Even Lord Ipswich broke off momentarily from recalling some of his favourite lines from the much-admired cartoon series The Simpsons.

"Your Highness, I have the honour to announce the arrival of the Minister Without Portfolio, Mr Peter Mandelson."

And there suddenly in front of them all was the most powerful man in Britain, the master manipulator, the Svengali of Spin, the Prince of Darkness himself.

They all gasped.

"It's frightfully good of you to come," said a beaming Charles. "It doesn't matter at all that you're three hours late. You must be terribly busy, running the country and the government and the Dome thingie."

Ignoring his host, Mandelson strode purposefully to the head of the table, placing on it a large, mysterious cardboard box.

"Talking of the Dome," he said, "I thought you'd all like to be given an exclusive preview of our latest model."

"How incredibly exciting!" said Charles, as the minister revealed a fragile balsa-wood facsimile of the now legendary dome, designed by Lord Rogers of Hammersmith.

Charles's adjective was echoed in a buzz of admiration round the table. "Exciting, exciting, exciting," they all said, from the distinguished Catholic novelist the Hon Piss Poore Read to the famous organic conductor T.S. Eliot Gardener.

Lord Ipswich was so moved that he immediately responded with some carefully-honed impromptu verses:

"There is nothing like a dome
Nothing in the world
No matter where you roam
There is nothing like a dome."

AS THE applause for this spontaneous tribute died away, Charles rose from his chair. "Mr Mandelson, ladies and gentlemen. May I take this opportunity to welcome our honoured guest who has graciously agreed to give us a full six-hour presentation on the Cultural and Spiritual Significance of his Millennium Dome thingie tomorrow evening.

"That will follow our tour of some of our magnificent Norfolk churches, guided by Lady Harrods. We're going to begin with St Candida's, Lycett Green, followed by St Paul's at Johnson-Up-The-Wall and St Melinda's at Messenger, with its incomparable double-rood screen, recently so sensitively restored by Sir Quinlan de Quinlan..."

As Charles warmed to his subject, his guests were so rapt in his monologue that they failed to notice a pall of smoke billowing out from the region of Mr Mandelson's much-prized model.

"Oh, bollocks!" came the unmistakable tones of the Prince's consort. "I seem to have set fire to the bloody ashtray."

Charles's eyes began to water as the acrid fumes engulfed his guests. This was not how it was meant to be...

Anyone not wishing to know the result should look away now

HUNTER

1815: THE NEWS FROM WATERLOO REACHES ENGLAND

How Cool Are You?

Do this test to find out if you're fit to live in Tony Blair's Britain!

1. Is your favourite film:
a) *The Full Monty?*
b) *In Which We Serve?*

2. Is your favourite band:
a) Oasis?
b) The Royal Philharmonic Orchestra?

3. Is your favourite novelist:
a) Nick Hornby?
b) William Makepeace Thackeray?

4. Is your favourite model:
a) Kate Moss?
b) Airfix's HMS Victory?

5. Is your favourite TV programme:
a) *The Teletubbies* starring Tinky-Winky?
b) *Civilisation* starring Sir Kenneth Clark?

6. Your favourite designer is:
a) Stella MacCartney of Chloe
b) Mr Wainwright of Marks & Spencer

7. Is your favourite artist:
a) Damien Hirst?
b) Sir Frederic Leighton RA?

8. Is your favourite team:
a) Arsenal FC?
b) The Royal Naval Field Gun "A" Squad (Pompey)?

9. Is your favourite Prime Minister:
a) Tony Blair?
b) William Pitt the Younger?

10. Your favourite media personality is:
a) Rupert Murdoch
b) Lord Reith

How you score:

All 'a's — Congratulations! You are Alastair Campbell!
Cool!

All 'b's — You're on the next plane out of here!
Uncool!

©Ben Elton

NASA REVEAL SECRET OF MYSTERY FACE ON MARS

by Our Space Staff **Adam Marrs**

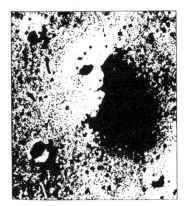

THE mysterious face visible on the surface of Mars has at last been explained by scientists working at the US space agency NASA.

Thanks to pictures taken by the space probe "Fuggin 7", the so-called face turns out to be a man-made phenomenon formed by billions of unsold copies of the humorous magazine Punch.

Waste of space

Said a NASA spokesman, "The magazine has been launched five times in the last 5 years with the inevitable result that huge quantities of magazine detritus have been dumped on Mars — creating this vast structure that looks like a face."

"Oh, and the ceasefire's still holding..."

◼ MARATHON TALKS END ◼

I could murder a McGuinness

I can see light at the end of the barrel

THE WESTMINSTER CHRONICLES

by Anthony Trollope

(adapted for television by the Daily Telegraph)

IN TONIGHT's episode the overbearing new Dean (played by Wesley Carr) finally overreaches himself by sacking the Abbey's saintly organist (nicely underplayed by Martin Neary). The choirmaster is accused of unspecified "financial irregularities" relating to the New Cassock Appeal Fund, the sum of 4/6 having mysteriously gone missing. News of these disturbing events in the Abbey Close is leaked to both The Thunderer and the Prime Minister (a somewhat over-the-top performance by Tony Blair). The Conservative leader sends his wife (a superbly frosty cameo by Cherie Booth) to confront the Dean at his "illegal" one-man Disciplinary Tribunal. By now the events at Westminster have become a major national scandal. Will the Queen step in and sack the bullying Dean?

Cast In Full

Her Majesty The Queen	**Prunella Scales**
The Prime Minister	**Neil Pearson**
Cherie Booth QC	**Frances Barber**
Dr Neary	**Derek Nimmo**
The Dean	**Barry Took**
Man In Pew	**Sir David Frost**

"Come on, let's have your report on bullying in the workplace, Fatty"

The Daily Telegraph

Est. 1855

Should Heterosexuals Be Allowed To Join The Armed Forces?

THE current breakdown of military discipline in Her Majesty's Forces, as evidenced in the court martial of the so-called Bonking Brigadier and the Randy Wren, is a direct consequence of the decision to admit heterosexuals to the ranks of the fighting elite.

Those of us who have constantly warned that such people could not keep their hands off each other and that it was in the nature of the heterosexual to jump on whoever was nearest have been proved all too correct.

Historically, services such as the Royal Navy have had a policy of recruiting only homosexuals, resulting in a glorious tradition of maritime supremacy. One has only to think of Nelson's order at the Battle of Trafalgar, "Kiss Me Hardy" to realise that *(cont. p. 94)*

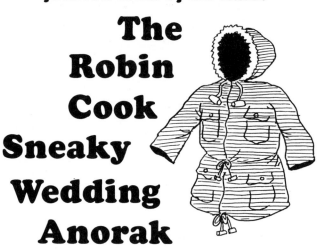

Spring Floods

From Sir Herbert Gusset

Sir, Today I was sitting at my study window looking out at my garden when I spotted the first bream of spring. It swam past the potting shed and nested in the seaweed on top of my car.

Yours sincerely,
SIR HERBERT GUSSET
Stratford-under-Avon
Sinks

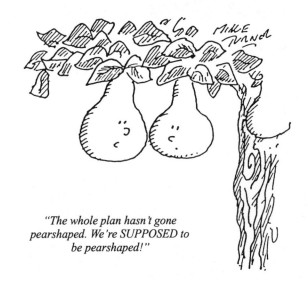

"The whole plan hasn't gone pearshaped. We're SUPPOSED to be pearshaped!"

PROTEST MARS TRADITIONAL EASTER CELEBRATION

by our Religious Affairs Staff **Sir Clifford Richard**

THERE were scenes of chaos yesterday when the Archbishop of Canterbury and a group of supporters stormed into the Cathedral during a traditional Easter Day address by Peter Tatchell.

The congregation gasped as Carey invaded the pulpit and attempted to deliver an Easter message about the love of God before being shouted down by outraged homosexuals.

Amazing Gays

Carey and his followers then began to chant christian slogans and songs including Hymn Number 94 omitting verses six and seven.

Said the Reverend Tatchell later: "It is a great shame that a vocal minority of christians should spoil it for the vast majority of ordinary gays and lesbians who want to celebrate same-sex marriage and a reduction in the age of consent."

Yesterday's protest by christian rights activists was clearly designed to draw attention to Easter, but Rev. Tatchell maintained his dignity during his ordeal keeping silent throughout except to shout occasionally "Carey! Carey! Carey! Out! Out! Out!"

"I do wish Witherspoon wouldn't keep phoning in sick"

NEW MOSQUE TO BE BUILT FOR SADDAM

Fire all minarets now!

SHOULD PAEDOPHILES BE ALLOWED TO ROAM FREE ALL OVER BRITAIN'S MEDIA?

by Our Paedophile (formerly News and Current Affairs) Staff

QUESTIONS were being asked by indignant pressure groups last night, following the release of hundreds of newspaper articles about paedophiles into the community.

"Are any of our children safe?" asked a typical parent. "I open the newspaper, turn on the radio, switch on the television, and there they are, large as life, in our own home.

"Why can't these editors just keep these pieces under control and out of sight on page 25?"

"It is a national scandal," agreed one childcare expert. "Our kids are these days being daily exposed to the most graphic and salacious accounts of paedophilia on every side, with no protection at all."

But newspaper editor Mr Kevin McFilth hit back by pointing out that "This kind of material fills newspapers and attracts readers.

"Any attempt to clamp down on paedophile coverage would be a gross infringement of the basic human right to make money."

LATE NEWS

Thousands more pieces on paedophiles to be released next week. *(P.A.)*

SALLY JOCKSTRAP
Winner Sportswriter of the Year

I AM second to none in my appreciation of David Coulthard, so I was delighted to see him coast past the post at Westminster Bridge in the fastest Marathon time this year — an incredible three goals to nil!

Jimmy White has had his problems, but it was good to see him make his name as a heavyweight by knocking out Chris Eubank in 3 hours 90 minutes. Now he can go on to bring back gold for Britain in the World Cup!

Talking of the World Cup, did you get any tickets this year? I rang Wimbledon all day, only to be told by some snotty woman who couldn't speak French that rain had stopped play! In the words of Baddiel and Skinner's hit golf anthem, "Men of Harlech in the hollow..." *(That's enough. Ed.)*

● *Sally Jockstrap is now Editor of the Daily Express.*

That University Challenge *Sizzler*

THE SUN's Ten Questions That We'd Like To Ask Britain's Brightest Blonde From M-m-m-agdalen Corr-lege in Sexford!!

1. Your starter for ten thousand pounds: *Would you like to get your kit off, love?*

2. Er...

3. That's it.

IN THE OTHER PAPERS

HOW the Sun disgracefully tried to exploit Oxford's Sizzling Egghead — full colour pix and interview by Glendana di Slaggiano.

"It's all in the Soaraway Sunday Telegraph."

The Life Of St Margaret Of Thatcher

by TV's Charles Moore

(What you will read exclusively in the Year 2007 Millennium Bug permitting)

Chapter One

And lo, there was a star in the East, and it came to rest over a certain grocer's shop in Grantham.

And the angel of the Lord came unto the wife of the Alderman and said unto her "Fear not, for thou art blessed among grocers' wives.

"For you are to conceive and bear a daughter. And her name shall be called Wonderful, Privy Counsellor, the Everlasting Thatcher, the Supreme Ruler of the Universe. Especially by Charles Moore." *(Not to be continued.)*

'RECOVERED MEMORY SYNDROME IS BOGUS'

by Our Medical Staff **Dr Spin**

HUGE numbers of people in Britain are suffering from false memories, according to Mr Tony Blair, the Downing Street specialist.

"It is a sad fact," said Mr Blair, "that too many members of the public remember the Labour party standing for social justice, equality and the redistribution of wealth."

Forget me note

"They are deluding themselves," he continued. "These recollections are entirely erroneous and are merely fantasies encouraged by unscrupulous so-called 'experts' using them to prove their own dubious theories."

He concluded, "The Labour party has *always* stood for wealth creation, private enterprise and an end to the welfare state.

"Anyone who remembers otherwise will soon find that I have forgotten about them completely when it comes to the reshuffle."

LOVER OF BLONDE WOMAN GOES HOME

NATION IN SHOCK

by Our Current Affairs Staff **Phil Space**

BRITAIN reeled last night after the shock announcement that the businessman who had run off with the blonde woman on television has decided to go home to his wife and children.

From Land's End to John O'Groats the nation has been discussing little else for months, and the unexpected fairytale ending to the story was last night greeted with spontaneous street parties, tears of joy and hastily organised services of thanksgiving in churches from Land's End to John O'Groats. *(You've done that bit, Ed.)*.

Said one overcome old-aged pensioner, "It's just like winning the lottery. I'm so happy for the blonde woman's lover's wife who must be over the moon after all she has been through."

Turner Prize Idiot

In a special statement issued from Number 10, Downing Street, the Prime Minister Mr Tony Blair said, "We have all been deeply moved by the plight of the blonde woman's lover's abandoned wife, particularly the episode where she wore the red dress at that party and danced around next to the blonde woman.

"She really exemplified all that is meant by Cool Britannia, and we wish her and her husband and children all the best in their new life without the blonde woman."

The Leader of Opposition Mr William Hague was quick to add his congratulations to those of Mr Blair.

"The reuniting of the blonde woman's lover with the woman in the red dress exemplifies all that is best about modern Conservatism — which believes very strongly in the institution and integrity of marriage. But since Ffion and I are also very much in favour of living in sin, we therefore have tremendous sympathy for the blonde woman in her tragic plight and we believe the hearts of the nation will go out to them all at this time."

Anthea Turner is 31.

MAN WITH FUNNY BEARD FOUND IN TOILET

by Our Showbiz Staff **Lou Dact**

Los Angeles, Wednesday

A man with a funny beard was discovered in a public toilet today. He gave his name as Stavros Tellysavalas Taramasalata. *(Reuters)*

"He had fleas"

Daily Mail, Friday, May 15, 1998

Red Ken — The Nightmare Returns

by Mail Editor
FILTHY DACRE
(£650,000 a year)

FEW PEOPLE now alive remember the nightmare that was London during the 1980s' reign of terror under the hated Communist dictator Ken Livingstone.

Red Ken. They were the two most feared syllables in the English language, bringing untold misery into the lives of millions of ordinary Londoners.

But then, thanks to the fearless courage of the late Winston Thatcher, the age of Red Ken was tossed onto the dustbin of history.

But now the tinpot tyrant is set to return, to swagger through the streets of London as Mayor, accompanied by a retinue of Stalinist newts.

Lest we forget, this was the catalogue of horror in the nightmare years of the reign of King Ken Newt:

● Billions of pounds of ratepayers' money paid to promote gay morris dancing and lesbian juggling in London's lavatories.

● IRA mass-murderers feted openly at lavish banquets at County Hall .

● Billions of rats set loose through the streets, as bodies remained unburied and mountains of rubbish towered over the rooftops.

● Nuclear-free car parks declared.

● Statues of Lenin in every square.

● Thousands of Conservative intellectuals driven out into the countryside to look for agreeable second homes *(surely "to till the fields"? Ed.)*.

● Tube and bus fares slashed to 10p (with special rates for students and OAPs) *(surely shome mishtake? Ed.)*.

You have been warned.

A vote for Red Ken is a vote for insanity and death. *(Will this do?)*

© *Alistair Campbell, an official Labour Party article.*

A Doctor writes

AS A doctor I am often asked: "Doctor, have you got any spare body parts I can have?"

The simple answer is: "Yes, of course. There are some arms and legs over there and a head in the fridge. Help yourself, they won't object as they're all dead. Ha ha ha."

What happens is that the artist, or *Sicco sculptoris modernis*, to give him his full medical term, is suffering from an acute desire to mess about with corpses.

The doctor, having trained as a medical student and done something similar during rag week, can find nothing wrong with this request.

He therefore tells the artist to take a couple of limbs twice a day until he gets arrested and jailed.

If you're worried about your remains winding up on public display, then so you should be.

© *A. Doctor*

GLENDA SLAGG

The Gal Who's Sexier Than Viagra!

LOLITA?!? Doesn't it make you sick with dirty old Jeremy Irons a-leerin' and a-peerin', a-moanin' and a-groanin', a-gropin' and a-mopin' *(Get on with it. Ed.)* over his naughty nymphette in a nylon nightie!?!! What kind of example is this to set to the country, Mr Toffee-Nosed Pervert?!! It's nothing more than a green light to Britain's millions of paedophiles! Give him a clap? Clap him in Irons more like it?! Geddit?!?!

HATS OFF to Jeremy Irons!!! At last someone has had the guts to stand up to the P.C. hysteria, the kneejerk moralists, the know-it-all do-gooders who want to ban a sensitive work of art exploring the complex issues of human sexuality?!?!

People who should know better are calling him Dirty Old Jeremy and Mr Toffee-Nose-Pervert! What kind of language is this to describe one of Britain's finest actors?!! It's his critics who should be locked up, say I!?

LIZ HURLEY — aren't chasick-ofher? Going to a wedding and giving everybody a peep of your panties!! For goodness sake, Liz, grow up!?!

THREE cheers for Liz Hurley for brightening up our lives by lettin' us all have a leer at her lingerie!?! And it's not just guys who like gazin' at her gusset!?? Geddit?! So they tell me!? They'll be calling her Les Hurley next!?! Geddit?!?!

READ Douglas Hurd's new book?! Me neither!?!

Here they are, Glenda's Full Maytime Montys!!
● ALAN SHEARER — I like a bit of rough near the touchline! Geddit?!
● DR MARTIN NEARY — They may not want your organ in the Abbey ducks, but there's plenty of room for it round at my place!?!

● HENRY DENT-BROCKLEHURST — crazee name, loadsamoney!! M-m-m-m-m!!!

Byeeee!!!

● Glenda Slagg has been appointed Deputy Editor of Private Eye. This complies with the new NUJ regulation that all upmarket periodicals run by middle-aged men *must* have as deputy a raunchy female columnist whose name ends in "a" (Christina, Petronella, Viagra, Glenda etc).

"They want another Dick"

How The Murdoch Press Would Have Covered That Murdoch Separation. What You Will Not Read

THE Sun

Friday, May 1, 1998   28p   DEDICATED TO THE PEOPLE OF BRITAIN

BLONDE SEX BOMB DUMPS AUSSIE PORN KING

by Our News Staff
KELVIN MCFILTHIE

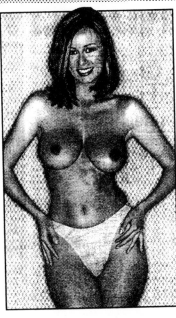

Gorgeous, pouting stunnah of the type Dirty Rupe is now free to go off and have nooky with.

THE WORLD's top filth merchant Rupe Murdoch, 68, alias "the Dirty Digger", has been kicked out by his sex-starved missus.

Busty, Estonian-born Anna (38-28-38) did not tell the Sun last night: "I've had enough — or rather I haven't!

"My old man's never home for nooky — he'd rather spend his nights setting up complex cable deals in Szechuan than coming back for a love romp in one of our luxury homes."

Black Underwear

The marriage first hit the rocks when Dirty Rupe left lovely Anna all alone in her Manhattan lovenest for weeks on end.

"I was so bored I took to wandering round in my negligée, wondering how to fill up my lonely hours.

"Then a friend said, 'Why not write a dirty book?' — so I did.

Steamy Sex Session

"But when I showed it to Rupe he was gobsmacked. He said, 'This is filth — I would not even put it in the News of the World.' No wonder I gave him the boot. What a bastard!"

Last night Mr Murdoch was unavailable for comment because we didn't dare ring him up.

THE SUN DOESN'T SAY

CLEAR off, you dirty old dingo. Get back down under where you belong.

Anyone who could ignore a gorgeous blonde sizzler like Anna, when she's clearly gasping for it, must be stark staring bonkers!

FURY MOUNTS OVER DANA WIN

by Our Israeli Staff
F. Yuri Gellervision and
Tel-Aviv Wogan

ISRAEL was split in two yesterday by the victory of transsexual pop singer Princess Dana International — "The Chosen People's Princess".

Secular Israelis are delighted by the breakthrough, but Orthodox Jews were up in arms (literally).

Said Rabbi Khillah, leader of the ultra right-wing Madnos party: "This is a day of shame for Israel. It was me who should have represented my country with my popular song, 'Smite-Smite-A-Smite'! I would have appeared with my backing group, the Israeli Army, and taken Britain by force." *(Shurely 'storm'? Ed.)*.

(Reuters)

EURO-VISION CONTEST ♫ ENDS IN FUDGE ♪♫

by Our Brussels Staff **Boris and Ulrika Johnson**

THE GREAT Euro contest ended in farce tonight, when the winning Dutch entry, *My Old Bank Manager's A Dutchman (He Wears A Dutchman's Cap)*, **was forced to share the prize with the French entry**, *Unfrere Jacques*.

The British judge, Mr Tony Blair, allowed the French to take the coveted Eurobank prize away from the original Dutch winner, after he had been pummelled to the floor and shouted at in French for several hours.

Winner Takes Nothing

There was confusion in the closing stages of the contest when the organisers first announced that for the first time Holland had been voted number one with an astonishing 14 points (the maximum possible was 15).

The French entry received only one vote, from the French judge Monsieur Chirac.

But the doors then closed and there were sounds of heated argument and scuffles lasting until 2 o'clock in the morning.

Waterloo-ser

The judges then re-emerged to announce that the Dutch winner was going to step down voluntarily after four minutes.

The French contestant would then be declared the winner for the rest of time *(surely 'the year'? Ed.)*.

Mr Tony Blair, president of the judges, was quick to assure millions of viewers all over Europe that this was "the best possible result for everyone".

Those Losing Entries In Full

● I Did It Third Way: **Tony Blair**, UK (nul points)

● Deutschmark Unter Alles: **Ex-King Kohl**, Germany (nul points)

● We'll Meet The Convergence

"The verdict," he said, "is extremely exciting and fair.

"The Eurovision song contest is no longer a matter of one country winning or losing.

"There is now a third way."

Criteria: **Dame Lira In**, Italy (nul points)

● Boom-Bang-A-Bust: **Abba Dabba Do**, Sweden (nul points)

● When Irish Ayes Are Voting: **Jimmy Joyce and the Dubliners** (nul points) *(That's enough rotten songs. Ed.)*

"I think we can take you off the all-fish diet now, Mr Isbister"

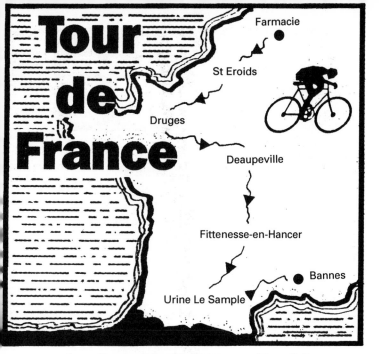

Tour de France

Farmacie
St Eroids
Druges
Deaupeville
Fittenesse-en-Hancer
Bannes
Urine Le Sample

Jour Quatre-Vingts Quatorze (Day 94)
Route In Full

"The weather's so unpredictable you never know what to wear!"

DIANA MEMORIAL TRUST SPLIT BY FEUD

'It's what she would have wanted'

by Our Diana Staff **Dame Flora Margarine**

THE Memorial Trust Fund set up to preserve the memory of the late Princess of Wales is reported to be riven with factions, splits and bitter acrimony as family members bicker over how best to remember the princess.

"I think it is a mark of the Fund's success," said Chairman Mr Anthony Julius, "that we have captured the spirit of her life at our meetings. They are full of tears, tantrums, wild accusations, half-baked ideas and broken marriages such as my own."
Lord Mishcon is 107.

ON OTHER PAGES

Diana's chauffeur's sister-in-law tells her story   **2, 3, 4, 5, 6**

Pin-up commemorative poster of Royal watcher James Whitaker looking very fat   **7**

Diana's bodyguard still can't remember whatever it was   **94**

Plus new tasteful competition: Eat ten tubs of Flora Lo-Fat Spread and win a white Fiat Uno!

NEW CURRIE FEAR SWEEPS UK

by Our Science Staff
Health-Scary Spice

THERE was growing concern yesterday that Britain was about to suffer a renewed outbreak of Edwina Currie, who had been thought to be "completely eliminated" after the scare of 1988.

There had over the years been a number of isolated incidents of Currie on Any Questions and at booksignings, but nothing on the scale of the previous epidemic, which left millions suffering from nausea and depression.

Many people were unable to leave their beds for weeks after contact with Currie.

Last week, however, scientists confirmed that Currie was once again threatening to engulf the country. However, a Government spokesman assured the public that they were not at risk from Currie provided they took sensible precautions, such as:
● **cancelling their newspapers;**
● **turning off the television and radio;**
● **eating huge quantities of eggs** *(Shurely shome mishtake? Ed)*.

COURT CIRCULAR

VANCOUVER
HIS Royal Highness William, Prince of Hearts, will today put on a silly hat and pose for photographs. He will be joined by his father, the Prince of Charlies, who will engage Prince William in some knockabout humorous banter.

The Prince of Wills will be attended by the Canadian Division of the Royal Groupies, including: Miss Patsy-Lou Moosejaw; Miss Emeline Lumberjack and Miss Daisy-Ann Beavertrap who will scream and present the Prince with items of their underclothing. The Prince will proceed to smile shyly and go red in the face.

In The Courts
The Case of the Spiggy Tapes

Day 94. Before Mr Justice Cocklecarrot

Sir Hartley Redface QC *(appearing for Mr Spigismond Topes)*: M'Lud, my client is one of the most distinguished composers and musicians of this century or any other. He seeks to injunct Mr Kevin Anorak of Crap Records (Watford) Ltd from seeking to profit from the copying, mechanical reproduction or sale of an electric tape recording made on 21 November 1961 in a hotel bedroom in Hamburg, when my client and his colleagues in the singing group, then known as "Spiggy and the Topemen" — later of course, as I hardly need remind this Court, let alone your Lordship, as "The Turds" — gave a rendition of a well-known song of the time, "Hugga-Bugga-Bim-Bam-Boogie" while in a condition of advanced inebriation, and while undergoing hallucinatory experiences in the company of a number of female admirers. M'Lud, may I at this point be permitted to allow the Court to hear the recording in question?

Mr Justice Cocklecarrot: Cer-

tainly not. We have suffered enough, having to listen to your speech.

Sir Hartley: I am obliged to your Lordship.

(Sir Spiggy was then called to the stand)

Sir Hartley: Can you tell the Court in your own words exactly what happened on the night of 21 November 1961?

Sir Spigismond: Certainly not. I cannot remember a thing about that night, or indeed any other. But it is not in the artistic interests of The Turds for Mr Anorak to see this tape released, without any royalties accruing thereby to myself or the surviving members of the most famous popular singing group in the history of the world. My accountant Mr Ernst Young tells me he has calculated that we could be missing out on artists' royalties amounting to the sum of no less than 47p, which to my mind, frankly, such as it is these days, would be totally outrageous. *(Continued Court 94)*

"Then Roger saw an article in the Telegraph about downshifting"

LASHING FOR KILLER NURSES

By Our Man In Jeddah
Lashtime O'Noose

TWO BRITISH nurses flew into Heathrow last night to face a ritual lashing from the Sun and other newspapers.

Their crime was to have sold their story to the Daily Mirror and not the Sun.

Said a Sun spokesman, "These two have failed to observe the cus-

toms of the country, and deserve no mercy.

"The age-old law of the land is quite simple. Anyone who is accused of committing a really newsworthy crime is duty-bound to sell their story to the Sun.

"If they do not do this, they face the penalty of a lashing of a thousand words, every morning for a week."

"I'm not religious in the conventional sense — I go to church"

AMERICAN WOMAN DEAD
Husband 'very upset'

by Our Entire Staff **Phil Space**

AN American woman who lived in Sussex has died in California (or possibly Arizona), it was reported last night.

As the news broke, the entire nation went into a state of shock, according to News At Ten and the rest of the media.

The woman's Liverpool-born husband was reported to be "deeply upset", in a statement carried on the front page of every newspaper.

The Prime Minister Mr Tony Blair last night broke off his peacemaking trip to the Middle East to pay a personal tribute to the American woman who was married to the man from Liverpool.

Lindiana

"Not since the death of Diana, Princess of Wales, has anyone commanded the affection of the British people like the American woman who was married to the man from Liverpool.

"She has indelibly left her mark on all our lives and stamped us with her indomitable spirit and her vision of a better, healthier, more positive Britain."

ON OTHER PAGES: Linda — A Life In Pictures pp 1, 2, 3, 4, 5, 6, 7. The Animals She Loved pp. 12-15. How She Changed A Nation's Diet pp. 16-18. The Linda I Knew by Glenda Lee-Mooney. What Happens When We Die by Dr Thomas Utterfraud. PLUS Hundreds of other Exclusive Features and Pictures exploiting the death of the American woman to the full.

The Daily Aitkengraph

Britain's biggest-selling quality daily

Friday, May 29, 1998

'How I Deserve V.C.'
War Hero's Impressive Claim

By Telegraph Editor Charles Moore

FORMER Cabinet Minister Jonathan Aitken told the Daily Telegraph exclusively today, "I had to lie in court or else the Germans would have attacked the Queen. I acted, as I did, honourably and managed to stop the Gestapo in their evil plot to overthrow the monarchy and install a puppet regime under Col. Gaddafi."

Mr Aitken, who has not spoken to anyone since his libel trial collapsed, chose to talk to the Telegraph because he knew I was a fellow Old Etonian and immensely gullible.

Said Aitken, "When I went to the Ritz Hotel in Paris, I was incognito acting for MI6. I chose the name 'Jonathan Aitken' to preserve my anonymity and allowed the Arabs to pay all the bills as a cover."

Aitkens' brief, personally entrusted to him by John Major, was to warn the Saudis about a plot against the Queen by Mossad, Iranian submarines and the IRA working in tandem with the hated Gestapo.

He arranged to meet King Fahd and sell him £1.7 billion of arms to help forestall the assassination of Her Majesty.

But the plot went wrong when Mohammed Fayed, who was acting for the Libyans, tipped off the Moscow-owned Guardian, urging them to sue Aitken for libel.

Once in court, Aitken had no choice but to force his young daughter to make false statements on his behalf.

The Telegraph says, "Jonathan Aitken is a fine and patriotic English gentleman. He deserves the Victoria Cross in recognition of his services to the country. Instead of which, he has been vilified and threatened with arrest on the grounds of perjury. Britain should hang its head in shame.

ON OTHER PAGES

Hundreds of other pieces about Aitken by various upper class friends and relatives.

'THIS IS NOT A PUBLICITY STUNT' SAYS WOMAN WEARING NO CLOTHES

by Our Entire Staff **Phil Space**

A BLONDE woman yesterday took off her clothes in front of the world's newsmen, telling reporters "This is not a publicity stunt, I just want my picture in the papers."

The blonde woman was wearing only a smile and the son of a former prime minister on her arm.

Revealing All

The blonde woman angrily denied claims that she was attempting to cash in on the fame of the former prime minister's son.

"He is only famous," she said, "because I have taken my clothes off."

"You would never have heard of him if it wasn't for me staging this publicity stunt." *Reuters*

On Other Pages

Pics of blonde woman with no clothes on **2-7**

Why oh why are we all taking notice of this woman with no clothes on? asks A.N. Wilson **8**

More pics of blonde woman **9-94**

James Major

How They Are Related

Emma Noble

James Major	Emma Noble
Earl Grey	Lady Emma Hamilton
Lady Jane Grey	Christine Hamilton
Major Ball R.N. Retd	Christine Keeler
Terry Major-Wogan	Mandy Rice-Davies
Cyril the Squirrel	Anneka Rice-Davies
Mrs Edna Kierans	Anthea Rice-Turner
Mrs Thatcher	Emma Nippleson MP
John Major	Emma Dale-Farm

FASHION CAFE

"Don't you hate the way they mentally undress you?"

Then and Now

1988

Major falls for publicity-seeking blonde

1998

Major falls for publicity-seeking blonde

Lives of the Saints

No. 94: St Paul The Flagellant

AND there lived in those days a wise man, florid of countenance, who was known throughout the land for his pious utterances. Not a day went by when his sermons and moral exhortations were not heard by the good folk of the time, who regarded him as truly the sage of the age. "Why oh why," he would preface his devotional admonitions, "must we tolerate the depravity that we see all around us? The whole nation sinketh into a sea of iniquity and licence."

And the saint attracted a great number of followers, including some of the holiest persons of the time. His acolytes included the Italian nun St Carla di Powell, the Abbess Lady Magnesia of Freelove and the Holy Father St Taki Takalotofcokupthenos, who had given up a life of crime to devote himself to sitting on a column in the middle of the desert (the *Spectator*).

And one day, when a certain pious man called Jonathan of Aitken was set upon by evil reptiles and robbed of all that he possessed, it was the saintly Paul who alone sprang to his defence, castigating the hacks with many a moral imprecation. This was an act of supreme self-sacrifice, for in castigating Jonathan's accusers, the holy man made himself appear most foolish in the eyes of all who saw it.

But his sanctity was finally shown to the world beyond all doubt when a holy woman came forward, by name Gloria, announcing that the saint had for a long time come to her privily, to be chastised for his sins. "Verily, I have been a naughty boy," the saint would cry out, "you must spank me on the botty and show no mercy." And so she did, belabouring him with rod and staff, before telling all to the *Daily Express*.

SPANKING SHOCK

No wonder I've got red cheeks

Arreshting Shtory

■ DRIVING back from a party, I take a detour to the police station, where I spy Police Constable Roger Perkins, son of Brian and Dorothy Perkins of retail newsagent fame, who invites me to provide a blood sample. He is accompanied by Sergeant Bob Harris, the brother of Colin Harris who is in charge of the successful paint department in the Sunbury B&Q store, who quips: "I don't care who you are, you drunken prat, you're going down."

Cell Shock

■ *To the delightful cells, where I run into none other than Jimmy McFarlane (of the Glasgow McFarlanes) who reveals to me that he will kick my fockin' head in if I don't stop whining and let him get some sleep!*

Shober as a judge

■ TO THE magistrate court where I encounter the charming Justice Melbury, whose Aunt Agatha Melbury is sister-in-law to Lady Bonjella Paget who famously danced with the Duke of Edinburgh at the Claridges Coming Out Ball in 1953.

He confides in me that I am a disgrace and should set a better example than driving about legless and being stroppy with policemen who are only trying to do their job.

The judge also has amazing news. I am to be given a huge fine and banned from driving!

P.S.sed

One for the road anyone?

The Dangers Of Genetic Engineering
by Charles

IN AN article in today's *Daily Telegraph*, Prince Charles warns of the terrible consequences of genetic engineering. "Look at this Windsor family tree" he said, pointing to himself. "If you try and produce a superior type of human being thingie you end up with some frightful freak of nature with large ears and a plummy voice."

"Stupid amount, stupid amount... do I hear ridiculous?"

Those Sinn Fein Demands In Full

1. The RUC to find new name to reflect its new role in the community, i.e. 'IRA'.

2. The old RUC to hand over all its illegal weapons to new forces of law and order, viz IRA.

3. Er...

4. That's it (for the time being).

"He's got his father's 'No's..."

NORTHERN IRELAND REFERENDUM SHOCK

It's all over bar the shouting

All sensible people are behind me

It's the hand grenade of history

"One balaclava, black... one Armalite rifle, loaded... Semtex explosive, 1lb..."

EYE REFUSES TO APOLOGISE

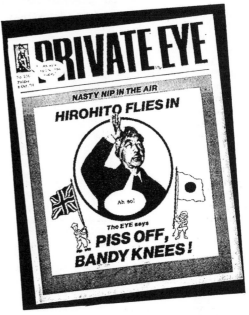

THERE are continuing demands from Japanese veterans of the 1970s that I should make some formal apology for the "atrocious" cover of *Private Eye* No. 256 *(see above)*.

Whilst I accept that the cover was regrettable and caused distress to thousands of Japanese subjects, it is not part of the culture of *Private Eye* to apologise (except when threatened with a libel action).

In any case, it is not possible for me as Lord Gnome to make any statement of any kind on a political matter due to my quasi-divine status as proprietor of a newspaper — a man revered as a god-like figure by millions of readers.

Besides, the events of 1971 are all in the distant past and it is now time to build bridges, not to mention cars, with our former enemies the Japanese.

And if they don't like it, they can refer themselves to the above cover.

Emperer Gnomohito
(Order of the Garter-Fuck)
The Chrysanthemum Throne
Ah Soho.

I-SPY

ENGLISH TRAINING CENTRE
BY VIDEO AND LABORATORY
FOR SD. SLTP. SLTA. AND UNIV.

WITHOUT ENGLISH

So...
Sub...
Ind...

Port Adelaide, South Australia

The Prince Of Wales Hotel
Camilla's Pokie Palace
PATRONS CAR PARK...

Enjoy Coke
Coca-Cola

ARRIVE ALIVE
Drivers Not Drinking
Last Week   7%
Previous Record 91%

Stellenbosch, S. Africa

Style Inn
Hair & Beauty Salon
0297 442750

DIANA
THE PRINCESS OF
WALES
WHO WAS QUEEN
OF ALL
HAIR STYLES
AND WHO DID SO MUCH
FOR BRITISH
HAIRDRESSING...

Shady Motors

Cairo

BAMBI KEBABS

Worthing

Pocono Mountains, Pennsylvania

ROPEY SERVICE →

Lyme Regis

Kuala Terengarau

WE MISS YOU PRINCESS DIANA
AND MOTHER TERESA

COLD BEER TO GO

Adigrat, Ethiopia

...ING TV PUPPETS STOLEN FROM CAR 334
...K CASHLESS WOMAN STRUCK BY MAN 335
...JOBS LOST AT GOVERNMENT OFFICE 336
...MAN MUGGED AT GUNPOINT IN CITY 337

Teletext

...AD END
...BLAIR DR

...d USA

Hague Dick

Fatal
RESTAURANT

QUEEN ELIZABETH
you must go to hell
MOTHER FUCKER SON OF A BITCH
GO HOME Fuck you Bullshit

Tokyo, 1989 visit of Duke of Edinburgh

RESTAURANT
CAN FART
BUFET LLIURE DE DILLUNS A DIUMENGE
ESPECIALITAT EN SANDVITXS

Barcelona

VOTE
BOB SLEIGH
CONSERVATIVE

Hampton in Arden, near Coventry

DOG SANDWICHS

Champs Elysées

GERRY ALONE
CONSERVATIVE

Winchester

RICHARD THICK
CONSERVATIVE.

Kent

Blairinroar 6

Renfrewshire

DIANA-DODI CORP.
Tel: (212) 529-2046
COFFEE DELI GROCERY FREE DELIVERY

New York

CASUAL
uni sex
ΣΤΑΜ ΧΟΥΝΤΑΣΗΣ

Karistos, Greece

TO LET
TO LET
New Labour New Britain

Winchester, Hants

in esclusiva PIZZA "VIAGRA"
al Ristorante Pizzeria - Bar "A CANNATA"
Per un mondiale più rilassante, più gustoso, più... eccitante.

Lipari, S. Italy

GORDON BRO
TAXATION SERVIC
PERSONAL & BUSINESS
ANNUAL ACCOUN
0131·552·22

FUKA FUKA NIGHT CLUB
TUBORG BEER

ITV

Was Fayed Murdered?

A Special Investigation by Fullcrummy Productions

(Sinister music. Film of cars going down Park Lane at night)

Nicholas Owen *(for it is he):* Millions of people all over the world love Mohamed Al-Fayed. But unknown to them there is strong evidence to believe that the most popular man in the world is no longer alive. And, what is more, he may well have been murdered by agents acting on behalf of the Royal Family and the British Government.

(Dramatic music. Film of cars outside Buckingham Palace. Close-up of policeman looking angry)

Owen: Tonight we look at that evidence and ask "Have the unanswered questions about Mohamed Fayed really been answered?"

(Film of bargain-hunters queuing up outside Harrods at the start of the sales. Cut to still photo of Fayed sitting in chair holding up copy of Punch)

Owen: We took this photograph to a French pathologist who specialises in looking at photographs of people who might be dead.

Princess Fayed

(Man in white coat appears holding up stethoscope to photograph)

Inspecteur Morgue: Bien sûr, Monsieur Fayed vive! Il n'est pas mort. Il est fou, certainement...

(A translator's voice begins speaking over the pathologist)

Voice over: In my opinion, this man is undoubtedly dead. Although his eyes are open, I can tell by the fact that he is reading the magazine Punch that his brain must have stopped functioning several hours ago.

(More sinister music plays over film of cars driving around Knightsbridge at night. Cut to man holding brown envelope full of money, reading slowly from autocue)

Owen: This man has never spoken before, but tonight he gives his eyewitness account of the murder of Mohamed Al-Fayed.

Man: I was driving my cab along Knightsbridge and I saw the late Mr Fayed walking out of the swing doors of Harrods smoking a cigar. It was definitely him. I'd have known him anywhere. Just as he was about to call me over, a big Rolls Royce drew up in front of him with a Union Jack fluttering on the bonnet. The Queen got out wearing dark glasses and pointed a Kalashnikov rifle at Mr Fayed. "Hasta la vista, Baby" she said and filled him full of lead. I swear that's what I saw I didn't make it up honest.

(He begins to count money)

Owen: But perhaps the most damning evidence comes from Fayed himself who is speaking to us live in the studio. Mr Fayed, are you dead?

Fayed: Of course I fuggin' am. I was murdered by the fuggin' queen.

Owen: So, there you have it. Conclusive proof if proof were needed that ITV really shouldn't be allowed to make documentaries — and that my career is definitely dead.

(Death March plays over film of Owen weeping)

Continuity Announcer: A five-hour discussion of issues raised by this documentary will be shown immediately after the commercial break. Speakers in the studio will include espionage expert Nigel West, Rupert Allason, the former MP turned espionage expert, Sir Bernard Ingham, Professor Ben Pimlott and a number of experts from the Broadmoor College of Clinical Psychopathology who believe that they are Napoleon.

Coming Soon

Diana — The Truth

2.30 a.m. C4

INCREDIBLE documentary that puts forward the astonishing theory that there was no conspiracy to murder Diana and that she died because Fayed's driver got pissed and crashed into a wall. Controversially claims that MI6, Mossad and the Teletubbies were *not* involved and that Diana is still dead. Unbelievable.

COURT CIRCULAR

Lord Bell of the Eighties (formerly Sir Tinker Bell) has announced the heraldic design for his new Coat of Arms. The coat will be held open, revealing a Membrum Virile Flashante, to reflect his early life around Hampstead.

The Coke of Arms will also feature a number of white lines (the traditional symbol of the advertising trade) with a twenty-pound note roulé protruding from a nose rampant. *(We've got the idea. Ed)*

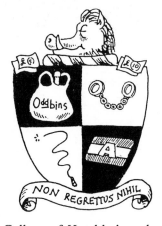

THE College of Heralds has also been commissioned by Lord Lamontable of Praed Street to design a coat of arms for his new status as Life Peer of the Realm. The design features symbols associated with Lord Lament's distinguished career. Central to the shield are an Oddbins bag rampant, a Visa card expired and a whip and handcuffs from his days as a landlord to Miss Whiplash.

A number of notes decorate the borders of the type that became worthless during his stewardship as Chancellor of the Exchequer during Black Wednesday. His motto "Non Regrettus Nihil" is an echo of his favourite song which he sang in the bath shortly before he was sacked.

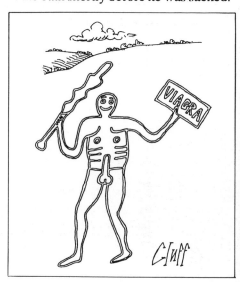

The Alternative Rocky Horror Service Book

No. 94: A New Form of Broadly Non-Religious Worship For Use At School Assemblies (as approved by the Synod of the Church of England)

Headteacher *(for it is he or she)*: Good morning, everyone. I said good morning, everyone!

(All may here make some form of inarticulate response)

Headteacher: We're now going to have our reading from something really important to give us a good start to the school day *(or they may use some similar words).*

The Reading

Sixth Former: Today's reading is from The Little Book of Calm. "If you look at the sky and it is blue, it makes you feel tranquil. If you look at the grass and it is green, it makes you feel peaceful. If you look at a plastic duck and it is yellow, it makes you feel good inside." Here ends the reading.

Headteacher: Thank you, Tracy *(or he may say Wong or Aswan).* Let's put our hands together to show how much we enjoyed the reading. And now it's time for a piece of music.

(Here he may play a tape of some suitable piece of popular music, as it may be Mr Michael Jackson's "We Are The World" or it may be Baddiel and Newman's "Three Lions On A Shirt")

Headteacher: I enjoyed that, didn't you?

All: No, it was crap *(or some similar expression of disapproval).*

Headteacher: And now, let us all stay quiet for a minute, close our eyes and think about all the people in Sudan *(or he may say Rwanda, Kosovo or wherever in the world there may have been a disaster reported on that morning's GMTV).* And now the dismissal...

(Here may be named those pupils who have been excluded for serious breaches of school rules, including murder, armed robbery, rape and drug smuggling. The students shall then proceed to their learning environment — or it may be the local McDonald's)

© SPCK (Society for the Prevention of Christian Knowledge)

"I hope I can rely on your vote on the big day"

"I'll arrange a lift for you on polling day"

Serialised Exclusively In The Sunday Times

JULIE

The People's Columnist
by The Late Diana, Princess of Wales

SHE began as a shy, gauche young girl with no visible talents, reluctantly entering the media spotlight as a writer on the New Musical Express.

But it was her marriage in 1981 to the glamorous Prince of Pop Tony Parsons which first catapulted her to world fame.

It seemed a fairytale marriage. Julie, with her winsome smile and

The official wedding photograph

leather wedding dress. Tony, with his white Ford Transit Van with leopard-skin accessories.

For a few years she could do no wrong. The world was at her feet. Columns, articles, TV appearances, books, plays, nothing was beyond her genius.

And how people loved her! Ordinary people like newspaper editors adored her.

It was said at one time that her picture on the front of a newspaper was enough to guarantee millions of sales for all the other newspapers.

But then rumours began to circulate that Julie was desperately unhappy.

She developed a severe eating disorder, wolfing huge plates of tiramisu and sun-dried polenta in the Groucho Club.

Julie Bullshit

And then the affairs began, often with the most unsuitable partners. She even gave a notorious TV interview in which she confessed to having slept with a woman on the Guardian.

But her public adored her all the more. In spite of everything. Perhaps because of everything.

The most famous woman in the world was at the height of her beauty, compassion and power. The Age of Julie had begun. As she told her confidante Lyn Barber in an interview *(cont. p. 94)*

On Other Pages

The Julie Burchill Tour of London — all the places associated with Julie's short, romantic life — the Groucho Club, the remainder bookshop, the Modern Review offices, the Groucho Club.

"Since it's so amusing, perhaps you'd like to share the joke with the rest of us"

A GRAVE CRISIS

This morning the people of Britain awoke to learn that their worst fears had been realised. For days the rumours have been flying thick and fast. But today it was finally confirmed that it was all too true. Mrs Geri Halliwell, better known to Times readers as "Ginger" Spice (see Spice Girls Go Sky-High, Sky 2, 9pm tonight) has decided to abandon the most successful popular singing group of all time. She is to strike out on her own in the hopes of establishing a solo career.

At this moment, it is unclear what has motivated Ms Halliwell to arrive at this momentous decision. Reliable sources close to the group suggest that there have recently been signs of dissension among the celebrated quintet over such matters as style, presentation and the group's future marketing strategy.

Alternatively, as Lord Rees-Mogg argues persuasively on the adjacent page, the resignation of Ms Halliwell may be seen as an inevitable corollary of the 20th Century's insatiable thirst for change, variety and instant gratification.

Certainly it is true that the pressures attendant on the life of a modern celebrity are such that it is almost impossible for a group of creative people to continue to work harmoniously together for any length of time.

Indeed, the path of popular music is strewn with casualties of this fearsome destiny. One thinks, for instance, of the departure of Miss Diana Ross from the Supremes in 1965. Or, more recently, that of Mr Robbie, who deserted his colleagues in the Take That. And there have been many more (see Sky's History of Pop, 9.30pm, Sky 1).

All of which makes it the more commendable that Lord Jagger, Mr Keith Richards and Mr Charles Watts have remained a cohesive entity through all the vicissitudes of the past 50 years, and remain to this day beacons of hope and an example of stability, loyalty and selfless dedication to a younger generation so sadly lacking in such role models.

Whatever reassurances we may be offered by the now sadly depleted Spice Girl quartet, the tragic fact remains that the group now face a future of terminal decline. In recent years we have become accustomed to the spectacle of our greatest national institutions falling into desuetude. The Royal Family, the Church of England, Rolls Royce, the BBC (see Sky Movies for latest premieres), have all been found wanting when faced by the peculiar challenges presented by this perilous transition to a new millennium.

And now another great institution crumbles. The world, we may confidently predict, will never be the same again.

♫ ...AND SO I FACE THE FINAL CURTAIN... ♫

FRANK SINATRA

RGJ

A Tribute to Prince William at 16

IS WILLIAM GAY?

writes Peter Tatchell

NOW that Prince William is 16, surely it is time for him to declare himself proud to be a homosexual.

There could be no more appropriate gesture to Britain's gay community than for William to stand up and come out.

It is unimportant whether William at 16 thinks he is gay or not. The point is that he *should* be gay.

The Next Queen

Indeed, for Prince William *not* to take advantage of the new legislation would be seen as yet another failure of the House of Windsor to move with the times.

Have they learned nothing from the sacrifice of Princess Diana?

Now that William is gay who should be his partner? *You the people must make the choice. Should it be:*

1) **George Michael**, the soulful soloist?

2) **Lord Elton John**, the Royal Crooner Laureate?

3) **Chris Smith**, Chubby Culture Minister?

4) **Ned Sherrin**, Radio's Mr Wit?

5) **Peter Tatchell**, left-wing firebrand and rather good-looking all-round hunk who *(That's enough. Ed.)*

THOSE PRICELESS QUEEN MOTHER LETTERS LOST TO THE NATION

Private Eye is proud to publish a few letters rescued from the flames of Princess Margaret's ashtray in which she burned an invaluable collection of the Queen Mother's personal correspondence.

This collection has been described by Lord Blake as "a national archive of immeasurable national importance" and its destruction "an act of vandalism on a scale unparalleled since the sacking of Rome by the Visigoths".

Clarence House, W1
4th Feb 1992

Dear William Hill,

I am sorry I have been so slow in settling my account — I have been very busy dealing with my grandson who is getting a divorce. I enclose a cheque for £2 19 shillings and sixpence which should go some way to settling the outstanding sum of £397,000.

Also, could you put £500 each way on my daughter's horse "Unlucky Jim" running in the 3.30 at Goodwood.

Yours sincerely,
Lady Celia Fotherspoon KCVO
Lady-In-Waiting-For-Result

Clarence House, W
20th April 197.

Dear Mr Thresher,

I am sorry I have been so slow in settling your invoice of the 31st inst. As you may have read in the newspapers I had a nasty fishbone stuck in my throat and had to go to hospital. I enclose a cheque for 2 Guineas and six empty tonic bottles (refund value one shilling and sixpence). This should go some way to settling my account of £957,000.

Could you drop round the following items:

Six Bots Gilbey's Jubilee Tincture (Export only)

One Bot Tonic

200 Rothmans (put on my daughter Margaret's tab)

Yours sincerely,
Lady Emilia Tumbleweed GSCE
Lady-In-Waiting-For Refill

Clarence House, W1
7th June 1965

Dear Mr Amies,

Thank you so much for the pink hat. I wore it at Ladies Day at Ascot and everybody waved. I loved the spray of plastic gardenias and the little rabbit.

I am sorry I have not as yet settled the *(continued p. 94)*

Let's Parler Franglais

No 94

Dans L'Inquest

Le Coroneur *(pour c'est lui):* Et maintenant l'evidence de Monsieur Fayed.

(Tout le monde dans le court rit out loud)

Le Coroneur: Silence!

Fayed: Tous les anglais sont a bunch de fuggin' snobs especialement Madame Shand-Kydd. Quelle fuggin' bitch!

Le Coroneur: Monsieur Fayed, controllez votre self, s'il vous plait!

Fayed: Forgivez-moi, Monsieur le Judge — je suis only un common working class man as anyone ici can voir. Unlike Madame Fuggin' Toffee-Nez qui est une bad mother, une amie de la Queen Mother et une fuggin' snob.

Le Coroneur: Monsieur Fayed, vous avez dit ca already. Donnez votre evidence — so-called.

Fayed: C'est un plot de l'establishment anglais. C'est tout ici dans le Punch magazine!

(Fayed exhibite un unsold copy de la humorous magazine Punch. Personne rit parce que Punch n'est pas assez good as it used to be).

Le Coroneur: Merci Monsieur Fayed. Ca suffit.

Fayed: Merci Monsieur Coroneur — et par le way voulez vous quelques emeralds? Tres valuable, seulement one owner, tombe off la derriere d'un fuggin' safe-deposit box. Nudgez-nudgez! Winkez-winkez!

Coroneur: Gendarmes! Arretez cet homme! Il est un fuggin' lunatic — pardon mon franglais...

© *Miles Kington 1961*

"Euston, we have a problem..."

"That's it! I'm confiscating that laser pen, Spalding"

FATTY SOAMES AT ASCOT

How about a spot of lunch?

It's only half-past nine

A Doctor writes

AS A doctor I am often asked by patients, "What is your success rate at this operation?" The simple answer is: "It's none of your business."

What happens is that the doctor, or *Medicus Arrogantus Masonicus* (to use the full technical term) suffers from symptoms of extreme short-sightedness and fails to notice that he is useless at his job.

Normally nothing happens and the doctor can lead a healthy medical life.

However, in rare cases, an inspection of the doctor's medical records reveals that he is dangerous and life threatening and has to be removed immediately.

If you are worried about your doctor, you should seek a second opinion from your lawyer.

© *A Doctor 1998.*

AN APOLOGY

THE *Daily Gnome* would like to take this opportunity to apologise to Miss Louise Woodward for its coverage of her trial for murder last year and in particular for the headlines "Why This Kiddie Killer Must Not Go Free", "Would You Leave Your Toddlers With The Nanny From Hell?" and "String Her Up Now".

These headlines may have given readers the impression that we at the *Daily Gnome* believed that Miss Woodward was in some way guilty of the heinous crime of which she stood accused.

However, we now realise that we have paid out a huge sum of money this week* and that there is therefore no question that Louise is entirely innocent of all crimes and is herself a victim of appalling injustice.

Tomorrow exclusively in the *Daily Gnome*

"My Hell In American Jail" by Princess Louise Woodward .. 2, 3, 4

"Why The Parents Must Have Done It" by St Louise of Elton 5, 6, 7

Free scented yellow ribbon candle for every reader! 94

Don't miss it!

E. Strobes
pp Lord Rothergnome
The Daily Gnome
Associated Criminals
The Old Festery
Kensington High Street

*We would like to make it clear that the Daily Gnome has not paid a penny to Louise Woodward. It has paid £400,000 to the Woodward Support Foundation Trust PLC, which is an entirely different matter.

"Our Father Ted, who art in heaven..."

Six To Watch in '98

Starburst (formerly Opalfruit)

THE **USA**'s six foot six striker has been given the job of putting the ball in the net. Unfortunately, his experience as a basketball player with the New Dworkin Aardvarks means he has a tendency to be shown the red card within minutes of kick-off.

Viagra

AT 65, the hard man of **San Salvador** is still a force to be reckoned with. Last played in the 1962 World Cup where he scored three times a night for the whole tournament.

Dabitoff

UKRAINE's exciting No. 6 shirt — with all stains removed. Dabitoff's extraordinary ability to knock spots off his opposite number's trousers makes him a hard man to mark.

Piriton

PERU's top sneezer has played a record 398 games during the winter when the pollen count is at its lowest. Famously cried for hours during the qualifying rounds against Holland, played in the middle of a tulip field.

Inuit

LAPLAND are expecting a lot of this 17 year old Seal Club player who only joined the national squad after 6 months asleep in his homemade igloo. Inuit admits that it may be difficult playing in Paris where snow in the summer is virtually unknown.

Al Fayed

CONTROVERSIAL **Egyptian** sweeper, who formerly played for **Haiti** but was expelled after offering brown envelopes to the opposition goalkeeper. His ambition though remains to play for England one day.

SALLY JOCKSTRAP

The Voice of Sport

THERE's only one winner for the World Cup this year: South Africa. Put your money on now, the bookies are offering 100-1 on "the Okapis" to take the Ashes! With players like Damon Hill, Emile Zola and Zola Budd how can they fail?

THERE's only one winner for Wimbledon '98 — and that's Greg Norman. The man they call "The Human Boomerang" has won every Grand Masters Slam event in the racing calendar. My money's on you, Bill!

THERE's only one winner for Royal Ascot this year — that's Martina Hingis on her Yamaha 750cc super bike. Vrmm! Vrmm! It's a hole in one for the Argentine showjumper!

A great summer of sport starts in September and you can read about it all here only in the Eye!

World Cup Match Preview

Group F
Serbia v. Kosovo

This should be a close-fought game with no quarter given by either side. Odds slightly favour the Serbs, with their Russian training and 400 tanks. The plucky Kosovans will do well to come out of this one with less than 20,000 dead. Watch out for big Slobodan Milosevic, the Serbian No. 1 shit (surely "shirt"? Ed.). He's known for his killer finish.

Group K
Eritrea v. Ethiopia

This match is likely to end in a stalemate. Their previous encounters have all been abandoned, after huge numbers from both sides have been taken off the field dead.

Group Q
India v. Pakistan

This could be the big one! Expect major fireworks when these two local rivals run onto the field and drop nuclear bombs on each other!

GROUP Z ISRAEL V. REST OF WORLD

(That's enough World War. Ed.)

WORLD CUP COMPETITION
SPOT THE BOTTLE

All you have to do is put a cross where you think Teddy Sherringham has hidden his bottle (or bottles) of lager. Mark it with a simple XXXX to win a night out in a Portuguese karaoke bar with the blonde totty of your choice and twenty players (most of whom are in the England squad).

Send to: "Spot the Hoddle Competition", Bottle *(shurely 'Bootle'? Ed)*, Lancs. Competition closes June 4th.

GAZZA'S UNPROFESSIONAL CONDUCT THREATENS CAREER

by Our World Cup Staff **Danny Halfbaker**

PAUL GASCOIGNE yesterday provoked a storm of fury when he went out on a four-hour "binge" of "non-stop football".

Gascoigne began by turning up at the England training ground with eleven mates and proceeded to run riot around the pitch in an orgy of passing, tackling and heading.

At one point Gascoigne was spotted unashamedly "scoring" to the delight of his rowdy friends.

They Drink It's All Over

There were immediate calls for his dismissal from the professional bodies representing cigarette manufacturers and brewers.

Said one senior manager, "Paul Gascoigne is a world class smoker and drinker. He is known as one of the top drunken oafs in the business. Why does he have to ruin his reputation by indulging in this weakness for football. He is setting a terrible example to yobs everywhere."

Lager Than Life

But top bender Coach Chris Evans defended the beleaguered Gascoigne. "We all know that Gazza likes a bit of football occasionally. But he doesn't do it very often and when he does it's not for long. Believe me he's still as good a drinker as he ever was." He continued, "Whatever the fuss over Gazza's latest football antics, he will be up there in the Pisshead's Pantheon along with such greats as George Best and Jimmy Greaves."

Gazza is 38 proof.

LETTERS TO THE EDITOR

Tragedy in the making

From the Archbishop of Canterbury and Others

Sir, We write, as the spiritual leaders of the nation, to protest at the dropping of Mr Paul Gascoigne from the England Squad. Even at this eleventh hour we appeal to Mr Glenn Hoddle, as a fellow Christian, to think again, and to remember the words of Our Lord that "There is more joy in heaven over one sinner that repenteth than over the 21 who turn up sober for their training sessions."

We remain, sir, your obedient servants,
†GEORGE CANTONA
†TERRY ELY
†LES GRIMSBY
†DAVE MACCLESFIELD
†SID GUILDFORD
†KEVIN WORKSOP
Church House, London.

Exemplary Courage

From Rt Hon William Hague MP

Sir, The nation must commend the courage of Glenn Hoddle in taking this courageous decision to drop the legendary Mr Gascoigne from his World Cup team. Such courage is the mark of true leadership, as I myself have shown by my fearless decision to drop Steve "Dozza" Dorrell from my own squad.

Yours sincerely,
WILLIAM HAGUE,
House of Commons.

Cultural Crisis

From Ms Deirdre Spart

Sir, It is sickeningly typical of the macho footballing culture that the so-called footballer Gazza should be dropped, not for his self-confessed and well-attested acts of violence against women, ie his estranged partner Sheryl, but for the comparatively minor offence of drinking alcohol and thus letting down his exclusively male team-mates. Once again proving that male solidarity is considered a more important issue than, er,

Yours sincerely,
D. SPART (Ms),
Hackney and Shoreditch Feminists Against the Countryside, London, E94.

Moore On

From the Editor of the Daily Telegraph

Sir, I would like to deplore in the strongest possible terms the decision to drop Mr Bamber Gascoigne, the well-known Old Etonian, in favour of Mr Jeremy Paxman.

This demotion of "Gazza" in favour of "Pazza" (to adopt the hideous vernacular of the young) can only be seen as further evidence of the complete collapse of standards in Britain today.

Yours sincerely,
CHARLES MOORE,
Out of Touch,
The Old Rectory, East Sussex.

World of Soccer
AFTER THE WAITING — ENGLAND COME GOOD!

by Our Man In Marseilles **Déjeuner Au Booze**
Marseilles, Monday night

THE WEEKS of training, the months of expectation, the years of careful planning, all finally bore fruit at 4.32 yesterday afternoon.

There had been fears that the England lads would not perform on the day, that they might freeze at the vital moment, and that nerves might prevent them demonstrating the sort of skills they have honed through years of weekly practice back home at Stamford Bridge, White Hart Lane, Goodison Park and Old Trafford.

But then, in the 38th minute after they had got off the bus in Marseilles, it all came together for England.

All those fears were dispelled.

The three lions on the shirt gave a mighty roar — as did our boys, as they charged up the street, setting fire to anything that moved and smashing up bars and cafes. It was enough to make grown men cry, as many did when the tear gas was released.

Kick Off Your Head

Our strikers excelled themselves, punching and kicking their way through the old town of Marseilles, as if there was no tomorrow. And the Tunisian defence had no answer to the English attack.

It was only when the French police blew their whistles, that the North African amateurs were put out of their misery (cont. p. 94)

A Cab Driver writes

Every week a well-known taxi driver is invited to comment on an issue of topical importance.

This week: The Problem of Hooliganism at the World Cup by **Reggie Boyz**, Cab No. 2-0 *(Shearer, Scholes)*

No. I mean, bloody disgraceful. They must be morons. Animals, that's what they are. Except that's unfair to animals. Makes you feel ashamed to be English. The sight of those brain-dead louts full of lager and singin' our national anthem. Makes you sick. String 'em up, mate, it's the only language they understand. Mind you, them Tunisians started it. They're trouble, aren't they, those Africans. And the French police aren't much better. Laying into our lads with their truncheons just because they've had a few bevvies and want to do England proud by singing God Save The Queen. Why shouldn't they? Bloody foreigners. They need their heads kicking in. *(Drives into rear of official London's Sightseeing Tour Bus injuring a number of Norwegian tourists. Sings "God Save Our Lovely Queen")* I drove into the back of that tourist bus once...

Next week: **Ms Beryl Queaze** *(Cab No. 36-24-36) describes how long it took to drive her family to Cornwall over the recent May Bank Holiday Weekend.*

Anyone not wishing to know the result should look away now!

DOES ANYONE KNOW THIS YOB?

Captured on a security camera, this is the snarling face of hate that is England today. This yob is part of a known gang of so-called football supporters who are in fact little more than vicious thugs.

If you can put a name to the face of Sports Minister Tony Banks, we will give a crate of lager and two tickets to watch England in the World Cup Final (Brazil v. Germany).

GLENDA SLAGG
Fleet Street's Golden Gal

OI, BECKHAM! Do us all a favour mate and string yourself up!! I don't know anything about football, but it doesn't need an expert to see that you've driven 56 million people into an early grave!!! Fancy lashin' out at that helpless Argentinian?!?!? Gawd alone knows what you were dreamin' of in your moment of madness, Mister Stoopido??!! Who do you think you are a-prancin' and a-dancin' and in yer silly red boots with your silly blond hair?!?!?? Here's Glenda's red card — and a piece of rope!! Geddit??!!!?

POOR David Beckham!!! Why's everyone got it in for him?!?!? All he did was give an Argie a little tap with his toe!!! Anyone would think he'd sunk the Belgrano (which Maggie was dead right to do in Auntie Glenda's book, Mister)?!!?? The one who should be strung up is the Dopey Dane with the weedy whistle?!!? I mean the ref,

stupid!!! Say what you like, Beckham did us proud and certainly added a bit of spice to the proceedings!!! Geddit?!?!??? I'm sure Miss Posh will when he gets home?!?!?

FAY WELDON Don'tchaluvher??!? She's the naughtiest novelist who had the guts to stand up and say what we all know to be true — a bit of rape never did any gal any harm!??!??! Wel-done, Fay!! (Geddit?!?)

FAY WELDON — Aren'tchasickofher??? She must need her head examined!! Fancy saying that women enjoy being raped!?! What a wicked witch who gives women a bad name and gives men the green light to go out and rape every woman they meet??! Here's a bit of rope, Fay — Rope never did anyone any harm (Geddit??), so go and string yourself up (You've done this one. Ed.)

SEEN Whistle Down The Wind??? Me neither. Great Show!!

HERE they are, Glenda's Golden Goolies:

● **LORD ALDERDICE** — Northern Ireland's bearded broth of a boy — I wouldn't mind an alliance with you (geddit?!?) at my party?!? (Geddit!!)

● **DAVID BATTY** — I'll help you score, Big Boy, don't you worry!! Best of 5?!?! Geddit?!?

● **BRUCE WILLIS!** — Demi Moore means worse!! (Geddit??) Come and Die Hard round at my place??!?!

Byeeeee!!!

NIKE PROFITS

MIKE TURNER

FOOTBALL TEAM PLAYS GAME

OTHER SIDE WINS

by **Our Entire Staff**

A FOOTBALL team lost a game last night, when the team they were playing against ended up scoring more goals than them.

The country immediately went into a period of official mourning led by the Prime Minister who praised the football team for scoring nearly as many goals as the team who won. *(Reuters/A.P.)*

On other pages

Read top football writers like William Rees-Mogg, Anatole Kaletsky, Mary Ann Sieghart, Peter Ridell and Peter Stothard on England's Day of Tragedy.

NEW LOOK QUEEN (contd.)

See the game? That ref was a bleedin' disgrace! It's got to be Brazil, though, hasn't it?

MAN WITH GLASSES DIES
Nation In Shock

by **Our Entire Staff**

THE whole world was in mourning last night after the tragic news that a man in glasses who worked in newspapers had died.

All newspapers are today filling their pages with glowing tributes to the man in glasses, whom they are describing as "the greatest man in glasses who worked in newspapers of this or any other time."

Sir David English was buried in Switzerland, for tax reasons

ON OTHER PAGES

BEAT ME UP SCOTTY

Star Trek: The Dark Side

PARLIAMENTARY DEBATES

(Han-z-z-z-ard)

Question Time

Ms Patsy Jacket (Billericay, New Lab): Will the Prime Minister please explain to the House how wonderful he is? *(Tory laughter)*

Mr Tony Blair (Sedgemore, New Lab): How dare the Tories laugh at that question. Can I remind them who won the last election, and by how much? *(New Labour cheers).* Thank you, Patsy. Next question, please — lady with the red dress and glasses at the back. No, not you Dawn, yours is tomorrow afternoon. Kim, it's your turn.

Ms Kim Blowse (Mothercare, New Lab): Would our wonderful prime minister like to assure the House that the questions he gets asked are not planted be careful not to read this bit out, Peter. Whoops, oh dear. *(More Tory laughter)*

Mr Blair: I would like to remind the House that I am the prime minister, not Mr Hague. And I think we all know why that is! *(Labour cheers, cries of "Labour's Coming Home", "Three Tonies On A Shirt", etc)*

Mr John Barcode (NatWest East, Con): Could the Health Secretary explain why, having promised that NHS waiting lists would be cut, his government has presided over an increase in the waiting list for acute admissions in my own constituency amounting in the first three-month percentile of this year to no less than 3,426 percent.

Mr Dobbo Dobson (St Pancras, Old Lab): Can I just point out to the honourable gentleman opposite that we won the election, not them, and it is hardly the job of the Opposition to ask questions of the rightfully elected People's government of this country.

Mr William Squitt (Baseballdon, New Con): Can the Foreign Secretary please explain exactly why all his junior ministers appear to have been lying through their teeth about the Arms to Sierra Leone affair?

Mr Tony Lliar (Sandline, New Lab): As you will notice, my Rt Hon friend the Foreign Secretary cannot be in the House today because he has more important duties to carry out, such as watching the Uganda match in his official bedroom. *(Tory giggles)*

Mr Lliar: How dare the opposition snigger? Don't they realise who won the election? I tell you, if we have any more of this criticism, we may be forced to abolish the House of Commons. *(New Labour cheers, cries of "'Ere we go, 'ere we go")*

Mr Paddy Ashtray (Pantsdown, LibDem): As someone who has recently returned from Kosovo, may I ask the Prime Minister whether he remembers who I am?

(House empties, as MPs rush to nearest bar to watch Chad v. Belarus)

Edinburgh '98

Your cut out and keep guide to this year's Festival highlights

COMEDY

St Magnus Linklater's Cathedral

Dead Cat For Dinner: Belfast stand-up Harry McTampax has reinvented himself for this 6-hour marathon monologue in which he pokes fun at the contents of his deep-freeze. Brilliant with hecklers, he once told a drunken lesbian to "fuck off". Unlucky not to have been shortlisted for last year's Perrier Worsthorne Award for Comedy.

ART

National Gallery of Scotland

The Vision of Jan Joop: haunting evocation of rural life in pre-war Belgium by recently rediscovered Walloon lensman Joop, celebrating his 104th birthday this year. In his foreword to the catalogue Joop explains that his 3000

pictures, taken with a box Brownie in 1928, were all shot on the same day, showing the same view of the same field. "After this," he continues, "I abandoned photography for my new career as a train driver in my native Bruges."

THEATRE

Lyceum

World premiere of **The Number 88 Bus** by discovery of the season Shoona McGussie. Set in a Glasgow DSS hostel, a schizophrenic lesbian baby-sitter hangs herself, after strangling the two-year old daughter of her gay neighbours, following the suicide of her social services lover who has drowned herself in her own urine.
 "Unmissable", *The Scotsman*

CABARET

Upstairs at McWong's Vegetarian Chinese Pizza House

Having A Ball: Terry Major-Ball takes to the boards in this light-hearted account of his years in post-war Brixton, working in his father's garden ornament firm. "One for the family", *Daily Record*

'CHANGING ROOMS' SHOCK

by Our TV Staff
Carole Silley

A MEMBER of the public broke down in tears yesterday when she discovered that a room she owns had been given "a tacky makeover" by a design team headed by Lord Irvine of Lairg.

The room, situated in a pleasant neo-Gothic building overlooking the Thames, belongs to the general public but was transformed by the Lord Chancellor into a hideous "Mock Pugin-style Folly" with "horrid wallpaper and ill-suited paintings stuck over the top".

The makeover, which cost £500,000 of public money, was a disaster and the ordinary woman was left "sobbing" at the thought that she had to foot the bill.

A spokesman for Lord Irvine said, "I am a friend of the Prime Minister. How dare you criticise me?"

THE Sun

Friday, July 10, 1998   28p   DEDICATED TO THE PEOPLE OF BRITAIN

Is THIS the most pathetic man in Britain?

Boris Johnson
Lightweight, blond interviewer, mistakenly allowed to meet politicians and discuss matters of state.

Ulrika Jonsson
Lightweight, blonde interviewer, mistakenly allowed to meet footballers and be smacked around.

Paul Johnson
Lightweight, red-headed lunatic, mistakenly allowed to be smacked on the bottom by blondes.

Frank Johnson
Lightweight, light-headed editor of the Spectator, mistakenly allows Paul Johnson to have a column.

Johnson's Baby Powder
Lightweight powder to put on sore bottoms (see Paul Johnson). *(That's enough Johnsons. Ed.)*

PAGE ONE OPINION

IT IS the question we never dreamed we would ask.

But we have been forced to think the unthinkable.

Is our editor David Yelland the most dismal creep ever to edit a national newspaper?

Just look at him!

Two days ago he said Tony Blair was fantastic.

Yesterday he said Tony was the most dangerous man in Britain.

What planet do you think you're on, Mr So-Called Yelland? The planet Moron? Or is it just the planet Murdoxxx?

Whichever it is, the Sun says "Get back in your spaceship, Baldie, and go home!"

ON OTHER PAGES

● We was robbed! — Sun World Cup verdict p. 6
● String up the ref! — p. 9
● The Belgrano Lovelies — Melinda Messenger and Co take their kit off and remember the night we sunk the Argies!

THAT STEPHEN LAWRENCE METROPOLITAN POLICE APOLOGY IN FULL

"We are very, very sorry that we have had to apologise and deeply regret the fact that we have caused ourselves such distress over the past six years" *(cont. p.94)*

LAWRENCE ENQUIRY DISRUPTED BY 'SINISTER MEN IN DARK UNIFORMS'

by Our Crime Staff **Ray Cyst**

A QUASI-MILITARY brotherhood of extremists yesterday tried to take over the inquiry into the murdered teenager Stephen Lawrence.

The so-called "Nation of Knacker" who dress in smart dark blue uniforms with identical ties made repeated attempts to pervert the course of justice.

"They are fanatics," said one furious court official. "Their presence here is helping no one. They have just appeared in silence in the witness box and looked menacing."

Non-PC

However, a spokesman for the "Nation of Knacker" said: "We have done nothing wrong. In fact, we have done nothing at all. That is why the killers are still free."

He continued: "This is a serious matter of racism. And we want to join in."

"I didn't know the nation of Islam had a branch out here"

NURSERY  TIMES

FRIDAY JULY 24 1998   *BRITAIN'S FASTEST-SELLING COMIC*

Wicked Stepmother Meets Snow Wills

by Our Court Staff **Spinocchio**

THE HEIR to the Throne was sensationally introduced to his future wicked stepmother yesterday over tea and crumpets in the Royal Palace.

Prince "Snow" Wills, who is known for his striking good looks (inherited from his late mother, the Queen of Hearts) was understood at first to be reluctant to meet the evil Camilla.

However Camilla, an older woman who is constantly told by her Daily Mirror that she is the unfairest in the land, reportedly got on famously with the young prince.

Contrary to expectations, the wicked future Queen did *not* offer the handsome Prince a poisoned apple, nor attempt to brush his hair with a deadly comb. Nor did she send him out into Highgrove Park to be murdered by the Royal Huntsman.

Instead the two discussed the relative merits of the Spice Maidens (a popular troubadour ensemble) and the All Saints (a similar minstrel troupe).

Camilla then offered Wills a Rothmans, and he invited her to a secret party for his father, Prince Charming-the-Press.

A Royal spokesman concluded: "It looks like a fairytale ending. Everyone is going to live happily ever after."

RAPUNZEL THROW DOWN YOUR HAIR!

"It's going to be one of those days!"

CAZ.

'WE HAVE DONE NOTHING FOR 50 YEARS' MI5's shock claim

by Our Spy Staff **Phil Bee**

IN A shock defence of its reputation, Britain's leading cloak-and-dagger organisation MI5 today claimed that it had not been responsible for the assassination of Harold Wilson, the disappearance of Red Rum, the sinking of the Titanic or indeed anything else.

"We are getting sick and tired," said an anonymous spokesman Sir Clive Postit, "of being accused of getting up to all sorts of skulduggery, dirty tricks and top-level surveillance.

"The truth is we have done nothing for 50 years except sit round drinking tea and doing the Telegraph crossword. By the way, did you get 5 across? 3 letters, starts with 's', ends with 'y', 'Man who sits around doing the Telegraph crossword'? Beats me, old boy."

Tinker Tailor Soldier Shayler

by John Le Carré On Spying

SHAYLER sat in the Bar Georges Blake in the Rue d L'Espion and ordered his usual.

"A pint of Boddington's," he said in perfect English, "shaken, not stirred."

Shayler looked at himself in the smoky mirror of the bar. No one would recognise him with his stick-on beard purchased from the famous Paris joke shop "Barbes Sont Nous".

"Excusez-moi, Monsieur Shayler," intervened the waiter. "There are some gentlemen who have come to see you from, how-you-say it, ze MI5?"

Shayler's face fell as did his beard into his foaming Boddington's.

"Hello, Shayler," sniggered Master Mole Catcher George Shmiley, "it's been a long time."

Shayler looked desperately for an escape — but there was no way out.

"Let me go, George, or I'll blow the gaff. I'll tell them everything. All the jobs you bungled, all the bombs you could have stopped, all the terrorists you let through your fingers. It won't look good, Shmiley."

"Too late, Shayler," Shmiley shmiled. "Everyone knows we're useless. It's even been in the Sunday Telegraph."

Shayler picked up his laptop. It really was all over.

"All right, Shmiley. I'll come quietly."

©*J. Le Carre 1998*

TOMORROW: Chapter 2, The Gadaffi Conundrum.

LET US NOT BEGRUDGE THE FRENCH THEIR VICTORY

by George Walden

S O THE French have done it — winners of the World Cup for the first time in their history. Some commentators have suggested that they may have been assisted by good fortune, but this is not a time for mealy-mouthed jealousy. It is an occasion on which to congratulate our historic rivals for a triumph which they shall remember for many years to come.

For a Gallic victory at the highest level was long overdue. Indeed France is historically a nation of underachievers who unlike the British, have had very little to cheer about recently. Not only do they have a stagnating economy, high unemployment and spiralling racial tensions, but they were also easily over-run by the Germans in the Second World War. Indeed, winning a football tournament may also go a little way towards consoling them for losing every major battle against the English from Agincourt to Blenheim right through to Waterloo.

And whilst Britain has given the world the train, the jet plane, the hovercraft, the television and the wind-up radio, the French have never managed to come up with anything more exciting than pasteurised milk! They are also a rude, obstructive and frankly rather unpleasant nation who are cruel to animals...
(cont. Page 94)

On Other Pages

● Did Chirac bribe the Brazilians?
● Picture of Bobby Moore holding World Cup in 1966.
● Depressingly Unfunny Cartoon of Napoleon in Heaven saying "I also could only ever win at 'ome!"

Late News
ENGLAND WIN WORLD CUP

T HERE WAS a night of national celebration last night when the World Cup was won by a team containing several players who play for English Premiership sides.

The team with the English based players was magnificent and thoroughly deserved their victory, which included at least one goal resulting from a move that had involved an English based player.

Following the presentation several of the pseudo-Englishmen were probably in two minds whether to brandish Union Jacks as they celebrated, before eventually opting for the French Tricolour.

There were further jingoistic outpourings at the sight of Englishman Reg Pritchard walking up the steps to receive his World Cup medal. Touch judge, or rather "assistant referee", Pritchard, having officiated brilliantly, later said "It's been a glory night for Britain".
(Reuters)

Exclusive to the Sunday Times

WAS RONALDO MURDERED?
Al Fayed's shock claim

T HE extraordinarily poor performance of Brazil's start striker Ronaldo in the World Cup final against France was sensationally explained last night by new evidence offered to the Parisian authorities by Mr Mohamed Al Fayed.

According to Mr Fayed, Ronaldo played badly because he had been killed the night before by a conspiracy involving the Queen Mother, the SAS, Mossad and Mr Tiny Rowland.

A Load of Footballs

Said Mr Fayed: "It is the only plausible explanation given the unanswered questions surrounding Ronaldo's mysterious lack of form."

He then listed what he called the "fuggin' facts".

a) Was there a white Fiat Uno on the pitch in the second half?

b) Who switched on the blinding floodlights before the game even started at eight o'clock at night?

c) Why was Ronaldo running at 4mph when his normal average speed is 120mph?

"The answer is simple," concluded Mr Fayed.

"The Brazilian offered a threat too the British Establishment because he was a foreigner who *(cont. p. 94)*

SUNDAY TELEGRAPH

Living In The Country
by Dominic Lawson (aged 12)

A YEAR ago we all went to live in the country, because London is very noisy and full of cars. The country is very nice with plenty of room for everyone, although there are lots of bugs and creepy-crawlies which get on your sandwiches. There are also microlites which buzz around in the sky when you are trying to write your column! But I still think the country is nicer than the town, and vice versa!

"There's one of those new 4x4 off-roaders"

THE NATIONAL
Diana,
Princess of Wales
MUSEUM AND GALLERY
OFFICIAL GUIDE

(all profits to the Earl Spencer Memorial Trust, Capetown, SA)

Room One — The Early Years

Exhibits include:

1 teddy bear, of the type the young Diana may well have owned, slightly chewed.

1 Hornby 00 Train Set, the property of Earl Spencer, with the words "This is my toy, keep off or I will burn your teddy" inscribed in crayon on box.

1 copy *The Ladybird Book of Nice Dresses*, by Roy Strong, inscribed "To darling Diana with love from Dame Barbara Cartland, Christmas 1995".

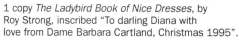

Mezzanine Gallery

A video will play on constant loop showing an 8mm home movie of the young Earl Spencer frightening his sister (age 6) with a dead mouse.

Room Two: The Transitional Phase

Exhibits include:

A number of coloured posters from the early 1970s, of the type which Diana might have purchased in her teenage years, showing Mr David Essex, Mr David Bowie and the Bay City Rollers. A recording of Mr Donald Osmond singing "Puppy Love" evokes the period.

Room Three: From Bride To Icon

Exhibits include:

1 Commemorative Wedding Mug, slightly chipped, bearing portraits of Her Royal Highness the Princess of Wales and the bastard who let her down so badly.

The Shoe Gallery

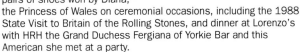

A collection of over 3,800 pairs of shoes won by Diana, the Princess of Wales on ceremonial occasions, including the 1988 State Visit to Britain of the Rolling Stones, and dinner at Lorenzo's with HRH the Grand Duchess Fergiana of Yorkie Bar and this American she met at a party.

Room Four: The Earl's Sister

1 copy of *Hello!* magazine, containing historic interview with the Rt Hon The Earl Spencer, accompanied by many coloured pictures showing the Earl showing us round his delightful home.

Closed-loop video recording of Earl Spencer's historic interview with TV's Sally Magnusson (generously made available by Lord Wahid Boy of Planet Street-Porter Productions).

1 photocopy of personal letter to Lord Spencer from his close personal friend Mr Darius Guppy, on lined writing paper carrying the crest and letterhead of Her Majesty's Open Prison, Ford.

1 stuffed and mounted head of Hackebeest (S. African journalist) personally shot by the Earl while attempting to restrict coverage of his divorce proceedings.

Souvenir Shop

Among the millions of commemorative items personally approved for sale by the Earl Spencer are:

- Novelty doorstop in shape of land mine.
  - "Fitness Leotard" bearing picture of late Princess.
- "Diana" showergel and conditioner pack.
  - Children's Aids-Ribbon tattoo set, fully washable.
- Matching Elton John wig and glasses joke set.

★ PLUS free scented copy of Daily Mail (choice of fragrances: Money, Money and More Money).

'THERE ARE WORSE THINGS THAN FAY WELDON'
Radio Times' Shock Claim

by **Women's Libby Purvis**

THE *Radio Times* **provoked a storm of protest yesterday when it claimed Fay Weldon was not the worst thing that could happen to someone.**

A piece in the magazine suggested that although Fay Weldon was of course shocking, unpleasant and deeply offensive, there were "worse things in life".

The magazine went on to claim that Jeanette Winterson, for example, was "infinitely more ghastly" and that "Let's face it, you've got to be grateful if you don't suffer from Julie Burchill."

But those who have experienced Fay Weldon reacted furiously claiming that the magazine was "belittling their trauma".

Said one anonymous reader of her work, "I can promise you that there is nothing you can imagine that comes anywhere near the horror of Fay Weldon. Don't let anyone tell you otherwise."

Fay Weldon is 68 and looking for publicity.

Panel 1: YOU'LL LIVE TO REGRET HAVING YOUR NOSE PIERCED, TROY. YOU JUST DON'T THINK DO YOU? — IT LOOKS COOL, DAD. ESPECIALLY HAVING ONE ON EITHER SIDE...

Panel 2: BUT WHAT'S GOING TO HAPPEN IN YEARS TO COME WHEN NOSE STUDS GO OUT OF FASHION, EH? — I'LL TAKE THEM OUT.

Panel 3: AND END UP WITH TWO HOLES IN YOUR HOOTER! YOU'LL LOOK STUPID, SON!

Panel 4: ESPECIALLY WHEN SNORTING...IT'LL ALL SHOOT STRAIGHT OUT THE SIDES... — SHIT. I HADN'T THOUGHT OF THAT...

Panel 5: THE MOST UPSETTING PART OF DIANA'S FUNERAL FOR ME, WAS ELTON SINGING "CANDLE IN THE WIND."...

Panel 6: TEARS WELLED UP IN MY EYES AND I HATE TO ADMIT IT BUT I COMPLETELY BROKE DOWN THERE AND THEN...

Panel 7: I KEPT SAYING TO MYSELF UNDER THE SOBS "WHY? WHY? WHY...?"

Panel 8: I MEAN, I'VE GOT A NEW SINGLE COMING OUT NEXT WEEK AND NOW IT'LL NEVER MAKE NUMBER ONE... — PAT PAT PAT

Panel 9: SO GARY, WHERE DO YOU STAND ON THE LEGALISATION OF MARIJUANA DEBATE? — WELL... ER... — ON AIR

Panel 10: IT'S A SENSITIVE SUBJECT AND I THINK THERE ARE THINGS TO BE SAID FOR BOTH SIDES OF THE ARGUMENT.

Panel 11: SO ARE YOU FOR OR AGAINST LEGALISING CANNABIS? — I'D PASS ON THAT ONE IF I WAS YOU, GARY. — ER... — TAP — P.R.

Panel 12: WELL, AS I, ER... SAID... — YOU'VE HAD IT FOR BLOODY AGES. TA.

Panel 13: HELLO CLOUDS! HELLO SKY!

Panel 14: HELLO BIRDS! HELLO TREES!

Panel 15: HELLO COWS! HELLO FIELDS! — AH BLESS HIM... GARY'S SO INNOCENTLY HAPPY WHEN HE'S LIKE THIS ISN'T HE?

Panel 16: OUT OF HIS MIND ON MOOD ALTERING SUBSTANCES? YEAH. — HELLO PEOPLE!

I'M SORRY I CAN'T BE WITH YOU TONIGHT ON THE FABULOUS OCCASION OF THE ANNUAL M.T.V. AWARDS...

I WANT TO THANK YOU ALL FOR BEING SO SPECIAL...

YOU'RE MY NUMBER ONE FANS AND I LOVE YOU ALL. CHEERS!

RIGHT, TIME FOR BED, GIRLS... DADDY WILL BE BACK IN THE MORNING...

WHIRR... EJECT...

ROSEDROP BUNNYPETAL. WHAT'S ALL THIS ABOUT YOU MAKING A BOY CRY AT SCHOOL?

HE STARTED IT, DAD. HE'S SO COMPETITIVE...

HE KEPT PINCHING AND TEASING ME SO I SAID "GO AWAY OR I'LL GET MY DAD ON YOU."

AND HE SAID "WELL MY DAD'S BIGGER THAN YOUR DAD, ANYWAY..."

SO WHAT DID YOU SAY TO THAT?

"NOT IN THE STATES HE ISN'T. NO-ONE'S HEARD OF HIM THERE." THEN HE BURST INTO TEARS...

ATTA-GIRL!

I WAS LIKE REALLY HIGH, MAN. IT WAS GREAT... AND THEN I STARTED COMING DOWN

NEXT THING I KNOW, I'M FEELING STRANGE AND DISORIENTATED... MY NOSE BEGINS BLEEDING THEN I BLACKED OUT...

YOU WON'T CATCH ME ON THAT POWDER EVER AGAIN MATE...

I MEAN, ALTITUDE SICKNESS! TALK ABOUT EMBARRASSING...

SHALL I START A RUMOUR THAT YOU'D OVERINDULGED?

NEWS: GARY BLOKE COLLAPSES SKI-ING

NOT ANOTHER CHARITY GALA DINNER, DEBS?

UH-HUH.

I MUST LOOK MY BEST. I'VE GOT A BIG SPEECH TO MAKE TONIGHT.

DAB DAB

ER... YOU DON'T KNOW WHERE MY FOUNDATION IS, DO YOU?

RWANDA, I THINK... OR IS IT BOSNIA?

I THOUGHT IT WAS IN HARLEM FOR DISADVANTAGED TEENAGERS. BETTER RING MY P.R. AND CHECK...

I MADE THE SAME NEW YEAR RESOLUTION THIS YEAR AS I ALWAYS DO... TO STOP THROWING TANTRUMS AND FITS OF TEMPER AT THE SLIGHTEST PROVOCATION...

AND HOW LONG DID THIS YEAR'S RESOLUTION LAST?

THE SAME AS EVERY YEAR I'M AFRAID.

NOT VERY LONG THEN?

NAH. ABOUT FOUR SECONDS.

YEAH. I SAW THERE WAS NOTHING FOR YOU IN THE NEW YEAR'S HONOURS YET AGAIN.

WHAT IS IT WITH THOSE BASTARDS...? IT MAKES ME SO ANGRY!!

William Hague says...

"THE Labour Party has no principles and no ideas. It's all just populist rubbish generated by listening to focus groups.

In the Conservative Party we do things differently.

Which is why we're asking **you** if you've got any ideas of what we should believe in.

For example:

● **What we should do about the economy**

● **What we should do about Europe**

● **What we should do about transport**

● **What sort of baseball cap I should wear**

We want to hear from you. Why not pop into your local branch of the Conservative Party. Or if there isn't one, you can e-mail me direct as squittcon@deadloss.co.uk.

Remember, you talk, we listen."

The Conservatives — The Listening Bank Managers

Report accuses Royal Opera House of 'arrogance and elitism'
— ● —
Report also alleges that Pope is Catholic
— ● —
Report further claims that bears may well defecate in woods

by Our Opera Staff **Val Kyrie and Dee Fledermaus**

IN A **sensational investigation into the bleeding obvious** (surely "State of Affairs at Covent Garden"? Ed.) the distinguished theatrical director Sir Richard Eyre has reached the startling conclusion that the bankrupt Royal Opera House is a large building that puts on opera and loses money.

The 994 page report which took Sir Richard a year to complete has come up with some revolutionary ideas to solving the current crisis.

Eyre on a shoestring

Sir Richard proposes that in future the Royal Opera House should:

a) continue to stage operas as before.

b) try not to lose any money.

Alternative Rocky Horror Service Book

No. 94: Service For The Induction Of The Hello! Magazine Into One's Charming Home.

Archbishop of Canterbury
(for it is he): Hello?

Reporters: Yes, that's right!

Archbishop: Ha, ha, ha. Do come in.

Reporters: Is it alright if we take some photos?

Archbishop: It is very meet, right and your bounder duty so to do.

THE TAKING OF PHOTOGRAPHS

(The staff of the magazine shall then process through various rooms of the house, taking tasteful shots of the contents of the Archiepiscopal fridge and other important but homely details)

Photographer: Can you lift up your eyes?

Carey: I will lift them unto the camera.

Photographer: You may now sit.

Carey: Even so, on the sofa?

Photographer: Yeah. Great.

READING

(There will then follow a reading by the journalist of a series of questions agreed beforehand by the Archbishop's press office. He may ask: "How long have you lived in this delightful house, Your Grace?" or "Where did your wife buy these charming cushions?" He may not ask: "What about gays marrying in church?")

THE DISMISSAL

Archbishop: Goodness me, is that the time? I have to be at Synod in 20 minutes.

Photographer: Just one more roll, your grace, and then I'll be on my way. Could we go out into the garden?

(The Archbishop grindeth his teeth but remembereth the importance of public relations in the Church of today and processes into garden as requested)

THE SECOND DISMISSAL

Archbishop: No, I really have to go. I'm most awfully sorry.

Photographer: So be it. Well, very nice to have met you, your holiness. Makes a change from Fergie, ha, ha, ha!

Carey: Ha, ha, ha!

(The photographer shall exit whistling some suitable hymn, it may be "Three Lions On A Shirt" or it may be "Vindaloo")

© Halo Magazine 1998

"We regret the delays and cancellations. These are due to the wrong type of people running the network. Thank you"

Dolly Draper, 17, partner in top lobbying firm NBG. Formerly editor of the influential *Prozac* magazine (prop. Lord Sainsbury), Dolly moved onto the inside fast-track when he worked for three weeks in the office of Peter Mandelson in 1993. Clients include United Biscuits and Allied Paperclips. Once boasted that he had Guernsey phone number of Geoffrey Robinson. Reputed to earn £850,000 a year.

Felix Mendelssohn, 23, Soho-based marketing whizz-kid of lobbying firm Mendelssohn, Mandelson and Mandelstan (MMM). Once overheard in L'Escargot claiming that he could arrange lunch with Margaret Beckett. Sprang to prominence after working in Milbank Rapid Rebuttal Unit. Clients include United Paperclips and Allied Biscuits. Estimated salary £1,050,000 a year.

Dolly Parton, founder of strategic PR firm The Parton Partnership. Formerly research assistant to Michael Meacher, Parton first went into business with fellow lobbyists Ben Lucre and Neil Lawbreaker to form BLT which was subsequently taken over by NBG (see above). She claims to earn £2,000,000 an hour.

The Eye names THE 17 MOST IMPORTANT MEN IN BRITAIN

WHO ARE they — the men at the centre of the cash-for-access scandal that is rocking Tony Blair's government to its foundations?

Oofy-Wegg-Tosser, 26, personal assistant to personal assistant to Peter Mendelsohn (see above). Once sent fax to the *Financial Times* leaking contents of Blair's lunch at L'Etoile with the CBI's Adair Turner. Lives with Molly Draper, sister of Dolly Parton and thus part of Blair's "Charmed Circle".

Ed Bore, 34, top aide to Chancellor Gordon Brown. Accused of leaking details of pre-budget discussions on public spending plans between Oofy Wegg-Tosser and Peter Mandelson to lobbyists NDC (Neal, Down and Creep). Described on Newsnight as "jumped up little pipsqueak". Married to fast-rising Labour MP Patsy Jacket.

Gussy Fink-Nottle, cousin of Oofy Wegg-Tosser, and member of exclusive Drones Club where top level political secrets are traded with the likes of "Bob" Wooster of Mori Poll fame. Gussy was once engaged to new Labour high-flyer the Hon. Lavinia Starborgling but the engagement was called off after an unfortunate incident involving the vicar and a bowl of golfish at the village flower show.

Dolly the sheep, 2½, widely respected "Clone" who has already worked as an adviser to Peter Mandelson, John Birt and Uncle Tom Cobleigh, the chairman of the newly merged United Allied Paperclips and Biscuits Group who have donated *(That's enough top men in Blair's Britain. Ed)*

LORDS REJECT LOWERING OF TROUSERS
That Debate In Full

Lord Backwoods: My Lords, the simple fact of the matter is that these homosexuals are utterly disgusting and what they get up to is pretty disagreeable. That is why it is vital that this House should not contemplate any further lowering of trousers.

Baroness Malaprop: My Lords, one of the essential freedoms of any civilised society is the basic human right of two consenting adults of whatever age to lower each other's trousers in the privacy of their own public convenience.

The Bishop of Sodom and Gomorrah: My Lords, some of my best friends have been arrested for their beliefs. If we reject this Bill we condemn thousands of young Anglican clergymen to a lifetime of celibacy. Surely it is time for trousers to be low-

ered for once and for all.

The Earl of Longjohns: When I was a boy in 1823 anyone caught engaging in an act of beastliness would have been thrashed within an inch of his wife. And it never did any of us any harm. Free Myra Hindley now.

Chief Rabbit, Lord Jacobs-biskitz: The law of God is immutable. As it says in the Holy Book of Leviticus: "He that lowereth the trousers of another man shall be deemed to have committed an abomination, and shall be stoned even unto death." I move an amendment that trousers should be raised at once.

(The debate concluded in an overwhelming defeat for the Government's proposal. The Trousers Bill was sent back to the House of Commons to be pressed for a third time.)

"Do you give Access?"

LAMBETH CONFERENCE MARRED BY TALK OF CHRISTIANITY

by Our Religious Affairs Staff **William Synoddie**

Lambeth Palace, Tuesday

FEARS grew tonight that the traditional gathering of the Anglican communion will be hijacked by bishops from the third world discussing God and other marginal issues instead of concentrating on the central themes of Lesbian Bishops and Gay Marriages.

Said one irate senior cleric, the Bishop of New Viagra, Arkansas, the Very Reverend Marvella (formerly Marvyn) Hassockburger, "We strongly *(cont. p. 94)*

DEMPSTER FLOORED AFTER 12TH ROUND

by **Ian Wooldridge**

LIGHTWEIGHT champion Nigel "The Pratt" Dumpster had to be dragged off his opponent yesterday when the referee sensationally stopped the fight after only two minutes outside the lift in the famous Daily Mail offices.

It was an extraordinary end to what was billed as "The Punch-Up Of The Century" — "Dead Loss" Dumpster vs. the unknown challenger "Who He" Helliker.

Hardcastle Much Better

Dumpster came out of his corner table at Launceston Place looking like he meant business. His face was red, his speech slurred, his mouth set in an ugly grimace.

"I'm going to get you, you bastard," he taunted Helliker who tried to duck and dive as the Punch-drunk diarist lunged at him again and again.

Then suddenly it was all over as the referee stepped in and declared Dumpster unfit to con-

He won on pints

tinue writing for a national newspaper.

On other pages

COURT CIRCULAR

BUCKINGHAM PALACE

Saturday: Her Majesty The Queen will today make a state visit to the McDonald's Fast Food Drive Thru Emporium in Neasden. She will be presented to the manageress, Miss Katie Wandulu, MBE, who will introduce her to the members of the staff who have bothered to turn up: Mr Wayne Mark, Mr Daryl Wayne, Mr Mark Daryl and new trainee Mr Nigel Dempster (one-star server).

Her Majesty will be supplied with the following Happy Royal Meal:

● One "Big Ma'am" with Queen-size fries and leisure drink of Her Majesty's choice.

● One complementary plastic Godzilla toy.

● One McDonald's "Duke of Edinburgh Do-Nut" with raspberry jam bearing legend "Have A Nice Day".

● One colourful paper crown presented to Her Majesty by Mr Ronald McDonald, CBE.

Her Majesty's official cavalcade will process past window number two and will suffer a short delay in the car park while Katie tries to discover why Her Majesty has been given "Nuggets with Bar-B-Q sauce" and not fries, as ordered. The meal will then be ceremonially thrown away by Lady Emilia Right-Fogg (Mistress of the Queen's Takeaway) and Her Majesty will return to Buckingham Palace for a proper luncheon.

"Damn soldier ants!"

START THE WEEK
with Jeremy Paxman

Paxman: Good morning. My guests this morning all have one thing in common. The fact that they are in this studio. We've got the well-known palaeonto-geneticist Professor Jean Drone, who has just published *The Impossible River*, a look at inherited speech patterns in Icelandic farming communities. The playwright David Drudge, whose classic trilogy on the class system *Shoot The Bastards!* has been revived at the much-acclaimed Ukrainian novelist Viagra Viagrova, who has just published a new anthology of contemporary Ukrainian verse. The Canadian installation artist Tammy Moosejaw. And to help me move the discussion along, the Times columnist Mary-Lou Useless.

So, professor, if I can start with you, who on earth do you think is going to be interested in this book you've written? It's 850 pages long, and it's unreadable.

Drone: When I first began my study in Reykjavik in 1958...

Paxman: Oh, come on, professor, Reykjavik for goodness sake. Couldn't you have found somewhere more interesting?

Drone: ...er...

Paxman: Well, if that's all you've got to say, then it's hardly worth coming in. Now, this play of yours, Mr Drudge. Isn't it just a waste of public money, putting it

on? No one wants to go to the theatre.

Drudge: I've always been fascinated by the peculiarities of the British class system...

Paxman: Oh, do shut up. This isn't the 1950s, you know...

Mary-Lou Useless: Could I just butt in here to ask Mr Drudge whether the character of the Welsh trade union leader was based on anyone in particular?

Paxman: Of course it was, you stupid woman. Everybody knows that. Who else is here? *(Consults notes.)* What's an installation artist, when it's at home?

Moosejaw: Well, Jeremy, when I began as an art student in Saskatchewan...

Paxman: Oh no! Saskatchewan! It's even worse than Reykjavik! And the other woman's from the Ukraine...

Drone *(overheard in background)* ...and the interesting thing about Icelandic initiation rituals in the fishing communities of the...

Paxman: ...don't tell me about fishing. If there's one thing I know about, it's fishing. I landed a million-pounder the other day in Broadcasting House, using this programme as bait.

(Enter Sir Christopher Bland carrying £1 million cheque mounted in glass case. Programme comes to halt rather earlier than expected. Solemn music fills up rest of slot.)

The History Of The Drumcree March

by TV's **Charles Moore**

1648
Battle of the Bog. Forces loyal to King William of Oranjeboom are routed by the Spanish Army of Don Portillo.

1671
Siege of Ballymurdagh. Orange marchers commemorating the Battle of the Bog storm the citadel of Bloddeegh Sonday under Dutch captain, the Duke of Bergkamp.

1701
Thanksgiving Service in Drumcree Church is followed by the burning down of the village post office (prop. Mother O'Carey).

1784
Birth of Ian Paisley.

1785
Paisley learns to march and leads Apprentice Toddlers through Catholic village of Armaghlite where they burn effigy of Pope Igniteus IV.

1786-1997
Annual March of the self-styled "Orange-Mentals" to commemorate the Battle of the Somme (*Somme mistake surely? Ed.*)

1998
Orangemen go through to meet British Army in final of the World Cup (*That's quite enough history. Ed.*)

©*The Daily Telegraph.*
Prop. Conrad Blackandtan.

Film Highlights

Reservoir Bogs

Let's go to walk, Mr Orange

WARNING: THIS FILM CONTAINS SCENES OF EXTREME VIOLENCE

JOBLESS FIGURES PLUMMET AS MILLIONS ARE LAID OFF

by Our Industrial Staff **Sir Keith Joseph Conrad Black-August**

HUNDREDS **more firms all over Britain went bankrupt yesterday, in the biggest epidemic of industrial closures since records were kept.**

But the Chancellor of the Exchequer Mr Gordon Brown assured the nation that there was nothing to worry about, since the Government's figures showed a welcome drop in unemployment to its lowest level since records were kept.

"This all goes to show," said Mr Brown, "that we have at last escaped from the old Tory cycle of boom and bust. Now we just have bust."

Our Economics Editor Sir Peter Jaybotham comments: At first sight there might seem to be a contradiction between yesterday's two sets of figures.

Yet when seasonal factors are taken into account, that is insurances, financial services and the like, we can see that, so far as the M1/M3 equation is concerned, Mr Brown is well on course towards his projection that by the year 2005 (*continued p. 94*)

"Right Mum. We're off to church"

TODAY IN THE NORTHERN IRELAND ASSEMBLY

Haghnsoaird

The House was searched at 3pm by the Traditional Procession of Sniffer Dogs and Police In Full Riot Regalia

The Loud Speaker (*Lord Manwithbeard*): Disorder, disorder! I call upon the First Minister, Mr David Trimble.

D. Thimble (Portaloo South, Official Ulster Unionist): This is a historic day for the people of Ulster. The days of division and dispute are at last behind us.

(*Uproar in Chamber*)

Rev. Dr. Ian Palsy (Anthill Central, Unofficial Democratic Paisleyite Unionist Voice of God Party): No, it is not, Mostah Tromball. You have betrayed and sold out the people of Ulster to the Devil Incarnate, Mostah Blair and his agent the Pope.

(*Cries of "sit down"*)

Palsy: No, I will never sit down with terrorists and murderers.

(*Sits down next to Mr McKillyKilly [formerly Brigade Chief of the Queen's Own Loyalist Paramilitaries, now Assemblyman for Dunbombin as leader of Loyalist Terrorists for Peace Party]*)

Mr Gerald Madmans (Semtex West, Original Sinn Fein): As the only person here who genuinely wants a peaceful and meaningful dialogue, I am now going to speak in Gaelic just to really annoy you all. (*Reads haltingly from book entitled "Bluffers Guide To Gaelic"*) Hondootedlaigh Mostah Tromball First Minister sinead o'connor seamus heaney a long way to Tipperary Mostah Blair brendan behan sean o'casey guinness is good for you kerrygold thanks to President Clinton some rough beast slouching towards Bethlehem to be born.

(*Cheers and volley of shots from Sinn Fein Assemblymen*)

Mr John Humourless (*Derry important, Official Moderate Nationalist Liberal Social Democrat*): May I congratulate myself on playing the central part in bringing about this extraordinary day of peace and reconciliation.

(*Uproar as Orangemen demand right to parade through middle of Assembly. 200 elderly apprentice boys in bowler hats march into room with drums and pennywhistles singing "Oranjeboom Oranjeboom"*)

THE INTERNATIONAL ENTERTAINMENT WEEKLY

WHICH TOONTOWN CHICK FOR DISNEY DI FLICK?

LOS ANGELES Stars of the cartoon motion picture industry were queuing up today for a chance to play Diana, Princess of Wales in the forthcoming Disney adaptation of her life story.

Top of the "A" list to land the plum role is Pocahontas, hot after her starring role in the native American spectacular *Pocahontas*. But also hotly tipped by showbiz insiders is Belle from *Beauty and the Beast* who has already played the part of a beautiful girl married to a monster in her last major hit.

Outsiders include Ariel from *The Little Mermaid* and long-shot "Anastasia", if the Russian beauty can be released from her Fox studio contract.

However, Disney have apparently ruled out Cinderella ("Too old"), Snow White ("Weight problem") and Betty Boop ("Still in black and white").

Other key roles have already been sewn up and whoever is to play Diana will have to fit in with a strong existing supporting cast.

That Cast In Full

Camilla Parker Bowles	Cruella De Vil
Prince Charles	Dumbo
The Duke of Edinburgh	Grumpy
Her Majesty The Queen	Ursula, the Sea Witch
Dodi Fayed	Aladdin
Mohamed Fayed	Jafar
Michael Cole	Pinocchio
Major James Hewitt	Hercules
Martin Bashir	Mowgli
Sir Robert Fellowes	Shere Khan
The White Fiat Uno	Herbie, The Love Bug

(That's enough cast. Ed.)

CZAR PAYS LAST RESPECTS TO YELTSIN

Text in full

"He was a sad weak man who should never have been allowed to rule over Russia. He was a remote figure who lost touch with the people and spent more and more time in the company of his beloved companion Vodka. DNA tests have now established beyond any doubt that towards the end he was completely pissed all the time."

Mourners at funeral

Mrs Molly Nargs (possibly the Grand Duchess Smirnoff of Warrington); Mrs Hiram J. Trump the Third (claiming to be Princess Amnesia); a man with a beard claiming to be Prince Michael of Kent, who was this year's winner of Russian TV's popular "Czar Lookalike" competition *(That's enough mourners. Ed.)*

MICROLIGHTWEIGHT MAN SETS NEW RECORD

by Our Aviation Staff
Allcock and Gordon Brown
(The Wrong Brothers)

A LONDON man, Mr Gordon Brown, landed in Sun Valley, Idaho today having established a world record for transglobal sycophancy.

He had set off from London on a historic journey, funded only by the taxpayer, in an epic attempt to suck up to Rupert Murdoch.

The previous holder of the record was a Mr Tony Blair who in 1997 flew all the way to Australia on a similar journey.

Louis Blairiot

Looking tired but triumphant, Mr Brownnose said, "I am delighted to have completed my mission. They have laid on a big reception of businessmen for me in their traditional shirt sleeves and they have all wished me luck on my return leg."

HOW BROWN FLEW INTO THE HISTORY BOOKS

Diggers Bum, Idaho

Downing Street, England

That Durham University Honorary Degree Citation In Full

CAROLUS PRINCEPS GALORUM SALUTAMUS
ORGANICUS AGRICULTORUM MEDICINUS
ALTERNICUM ET CARBUNCULUS
STRUCTORES INTERLOCUTUS AD FLORUM ET
ARBORUM LUNATICUS AMATOR NEDDIUS
SEEGOONIS ET MILLIGANIS PINGENDO AQUA
COLORIBUS PISSPOORUS CUM SCRIBENDO
HORRIBILIS LIVRIS PUERILIS SENEX
LOCHNAGARE ETCETERA PARTNERUS
INTIMATUS FORNICATUS CAMILLA TAMPAX
VOBISCUM *(CONTINUENDUM AD PAGINA XCIV)*

HOW COULD THEY LET IT HAPPEN?

Storm Grows Over Prince's Safety Blunder

by Jacob and Wilhelm Grimm

SAFETY EXPERTS were appalled yesterday when they saw pictures of a young prince climbing a sheer 170-foot tower, relying for support only on the hair of a teenage girl.

A passing wood engraver caught the horrifying scene as the young man began his ascent of the tower — without a safety harness, a hard hat, a parachute, a safety net or any of the other items of equipment that experts now regard as essential to anyone attempting a climb of more than 1.4 metres above the ground.

HAIR-RAISING TALE

This was the timetable of horror that has shocked the world:

3.42 p.m. Prince arrives at tower.

3.43 p.m. A young girl, whose name cannot be revealed for legal reasons, lets down a strand of her golden locks from the room at the top of the tower where she had been held in close confinement for twelve years.

3.45 p.m. The prince begins his reckless ascent without a proper safety line or any of the other devices listed above.

3.52 p.m. The prince completes climb.

IT'S A RAP-UNZEL

Last night Palace sources revealed that the Prince's father, King Carbuncle, was "absolutely livid" when he heard of his son's flagrant breach of basic safety rules.

We understand that much of the blame for this incident which has shocked the world attaches to the Prince's guardian, Ms Tiggy Winkle, 46, an elderly hedgehog who could now face dismissal for failing to ensure that the Prince complied with the EC's Personal Protective Equipment (Safety Helmets) Directive 90/46.

Said a spokesman for the Fairyland School of Outward Bound Hairclimbing and Beanstalking: "This was an accident waiting to happen, even though it didn't."

STOP PRESS

Last night it was reported that the mystery blonde in the Royal hairclimbing scandal, a Miss Rapunzel, 18, had been taken into care by social workers.

The Abseiling Prince

IRA CONDEMNS IRA
Adams Lashes Terrorists

by Our Northern Ireland Staff **Lunchtime O'Magh**

IN A dramatic announcement that shocked himself, Mr Gerald Manley Adams, the writer and statesman, last night hit out at the "depraved killers" behind the Omagh bomb outrage.

"What sort of people plant a bomb in a busy shopping street in order to kill innocent women and children?" he asked.

Mr Adams was among the 50,000 mourners who yesterday packed the streets of the small Ulster market town.

McGuinness Is Bad For You

With tears streaming down his face, he told reporters: "If these cowardly murderers think they can advance their cause by killing people, they're probably right."

(Reuters)

"I'm in the beautiful pea-green boat right now, so I'll be there in about ten minutes…"

YELTSIN — CRISIS DEEPENS

I'm losing my roubles

Is This The World's Most Dangerous Man?

by Our Insight Team
Phil Space and Philippa Page

WESTERN intelligence experts now believe that the biggest threat to world peace is a man named Abu Bil Clintstone, who spends his life holed up in a lavishly equipped overground bunker somewhere in North America, plotting indiscriminate bombings all around the world.

A devout non-Moslem, Clintstone is said by defence analysts to surround himself with beautiful women who fuel his fantasies of power and world domination.

Satellite pictures taken from CNN reveal the arch-terrorist's hidden multi-billion dollar fortress to be situated in a leafy suburb of downtown Washington, D.C.

Clintstone is guarded night and day by heavily armed fanatics who believe in his vision of a world controlled by the will of one man and his dream of pan-Clintstonism.

Osama Time And The Living Is Sleazy

There he sits in his so-called "oval office" poring over maps and ordering lightning strikes on "soft targets" throughout the world.

Today it may be a training camp in Afghanistan, tomorrow it may be Boots the Chemists in faraway Neasden.

Make no mistake, the world will never be a safe place while the President of the United States is still at large.

World of Sock-Her

GAZZA DROPPED FROM MARRIAGE

by Our Football Staff
Dee Vorce and Ali Money

SOCCER star Paul Gascoigne was yesterday dropped from his marriage, in a shock decision that outraged his fans throughout the country (Chris Evans and Danny Baker).

Gascoigne was accused by his boss Mrs Shezza Gascoigne of:
● staying out late getting drunk
● not turning up for marital sessions
● unprofessional conduct on and off the bed
● going for the woman rather than the ball. *(That's enough accusations. Ed.)*

Said one commentator, however, "Gazza is still a young man in marriage terms. He has years of husbandry ahead of him, providing he is given the right sort of coaching."

The marriage was dissolved in several pints of lager.

THE TIMETABLE OF TERROR THAT ROCKED THE WORLD

THE EYE'S AT-A-GLANCE GUIDE TO THE WORLD'S WORST CRISIS SINCE CUBA 1962

Monday 23 August

6.31 pm Huge bombs hit U.S. Embassies in Africa.

6.32 pm Monica Lewinsky gets into taxi showing knees.

6.33 pm Prosecutor Starr announces impeachment of President "imminent".

6.34 pm President launches enormous missile attack at "hostile targets" in Afghanistan and Khartoum.

6.36 pm Tony Blair sees attack on TV and rushes to support the President's action as "legitimate self-defence in accordance with Chapter 279 of the UN Charter".

6.40 pm President appears on television in military uniform and confesses to "appropriate bombing behaviour". "It was self-defence," he explains. "We must stand up to these unprovoked attacks by Prosecutor Stan." Marine band plays "God Bless America" and "The Starr and Strips".

6.43 pm First cruise missile hits Monica Lewinsky.
(That's enough timetable of terror. Ed.)

IT LOOKS LIKE IMPEACHMENT!

HMM... I'VE NEVER TRIED IT WITH A PEACH!

YABBA DABBA DNA!

DIANA – ONE YEAR ON

A YEAR ago we asked our columnist **Phil Space** to fill up some space with a piece about the Death of Diana, Princess of Wales. A year on we are asking him to do the same thing — except to make it even longer. Here is his moving account of his feelings on hearing the news that he had to write another 5,000 words by this afternoon.

Grief. Sadness. Sorrow. Heartache. Despair. I used all these words exactly a year ago on the fateful day when the editor asked me to fill up some space. I am reminded of them again a year on when I once more have to confront my own emotions at the prospect of working through my lunch break to churn out some lachrymose pile of (continued pages 94, 95, 96 etc)

Has Death Changed Diana?

by Antonia Holden, John Mortiboys, A.N. Wislon, Lynda Lee-Slagg and millions more

IT IS EXACTLY 365 days since the event that changed the nation irrevocably.

Britain turned overnight from being a repressed, uncaring, stuffy, class-ridden... bowler hats... warm beer... to a caring, sharing, compassionate society... in touch with feminine side... renewed sense of religious purpose... land mines... aromatherapy... Age of Aquarius... new millennium.

And yet a year later how has the shining icon who was at the centre of the emotional earthquake really changed?

Who can say?

One thing is certain. Britain is a changed place... Prince Charles very popular... Queen doing a great job... Queen Mother God bless her... monarchy reinvigorated... memorial garden not such a good idea after all. *(Will this do? A.H.) (Yes, but lots more please tomorrow. Ed.)*

FAYED BLAMES OWNER OF RITZ FOR TRAGEDY

*by Our Man on the Champs Elysee **Matthew Parris** (and his Mum)*

IN AN astonishing new twist to the long-running controversy over the death of Diana, the Princess of Wales, Mr Mohamed Al Fayed has launched a bitter attack on the owner of the Ritz Hotel in Paris, who he claims is a "fuggin' idiot".

"This man," he told the French magistrate through his letterbox at 3 o'clock in the morning, "allowed the most beautiful woman in the world to be driven home from his hotel by one of his drunken employees.

"And then he had the fuggin' nerve to blame it all on the Queen of England, the fuggin' bitch.

"No wonder they won't give him a fuggin' passport. He's a fuggin' lunatic, I tell you."

Mr Fayed then offered a £100 million reward for his own arrest but lawyers acting for Mr Fayed furiously denied Mr Fayed's allegations and immediately served writs for defamation on themselves.

TEN TELL-TALE SIGNS THAT THE MONARCHY HAS CHANGED FOR EVER

1. The Queen was seen in a shop that sells "trainers".

2. The Royal Standard was seen flying at half-mast over Windsor when the Queen Mother's horse, Large One, came last in a claiming stakes at Uttoxeter.

3. Prince Charles has been seen openly smiling at his sons at a Spice Girls' concert in Moosejaw, Canada.

4. Gentlemen attending this year's Buckingham Palace Garden Parties were no longer required to wear moustaches.

5. The Queen personally met a woman with pink hair and a nose stud (possibly her niece).

6. No traitors were executed during the August Bank Holiday weekend.

7. Er...

8. That's it.

On other pages

"It's a minefield!"

Where Were You When You Heard The News?

EVERYONE in the world remembers exactly where they were when they heard the tragic news of Diana's death.

It being a bank holiday weekend, we rang round a selection of anyone famous who was at home, asking them to relive those dreadful moments on August 31 1997.

TREVOR REES-JONES, bodyguard to the late Diana, Princess of Wales: "I can't remember." *(Continued on all other pages)*

Very Important Changes to Private Eye Scheduling

Private Eye is pleased to announce a major shake-up of its scheduling, after six months consultation with focus groups in all parts of the country.

As from midnight tonight, the following alterations will apply:

■ **Page One will remain in its old position, although it will be extended onto page two.**

■ **Page Two will be shortened and moved to its new slot on page eight.**

■ **Page Seven is coming to an end, to be replaced by a revamped page ten, which will in future be known by a new title as "Page Nine".**

■ **The popular Page Eleven is to be closed down.**

■ **Pages Fourteen-Eighteen will be available only on the Internet at www.radiofour.co.uk**

■ **Page Nineteen will split in two. The top half will be available only to readers in Scotland. The bottom half will be available to no one.**

We are extremely keen to know our readers' views on these changes. Please will you fill in the form below as soon as possible.

The new schedule is:

☐ Much more accessible and user-friendly

☐ Brilliant

☐ A work of genius

The Eye — you make it what it is